Frank Foxcroft, Andrew P. Peabody

Resurgit

a collection of hymns and songs of the resurrection

Frank Foxcroft, Andrew P. Peabody

Resurgit
a collection of hymns and songs of the resurrection

ISBN/EAN: 9783741193569

Manufactured in Europe, USA, Canada, Australia, Japa

Cover: Foto ©ninafisch / pixelio.de

Manufactured and distributed by brebook publishing software (www.brebook.com)

Frank Foxcroft, Andrew P. Peabody

Resurgit

Table of Contents.

PREFATORY NOTE	v
INDEX OF FIRST LINES	ix
INDEX OF LATIN HYMNS	xv
INDEX OF AUTHORS	xvii
INDEX OF TRANSLATORS	xxi
INTRODUCTION BY ANDREW P. PEABODY, D.D.	xxiii
HYMNS FROM THE GREEK	1
HYMNS FROM THE LATIN	25
HYMNS FROM THE RUSSIAN	97
HYMNS FROM THE DANISH	101
HYMNS FROM THE GERMAN	109
HYMNS FROM THE SWEDISH	159
ENGLISH HYMNS	167
AMERICAN HYMNS	311
BIBLIOGRAPHY	347

Prefatory Note.

THE present volume explains, and, it may be hoped, justifies itself. It is the result of a more careful search than has been hitherto made in the rich field of resurrection-poetry. It finds its purpose in a desire to contribute to the observance of a day, the hopes and associations of which are precious to all branches of the Christian Church; and, besides this, to present a collection of verse sufficiently varied and suggestive to be welcome not only at Easter-time, but throughout the year. For the Christian Sabbath is itself a weekly commemoration of the rising of Christ, and we do not wisely if we keep the Easter-feast but once a year.

The scope of the volume might have been greatly enlarged by including poems relating to the ascension and exaltation of Christ, or to the general resurrection, and the joys of heaven. Poems of both these classes are often included among Easter-pieces. But, if these had been taken, the collection would have lost its distinctive character. With a very few exceptions, the poems which it contains relate directly to the rising of Christ, and to the Christian hope of resurrection as based thereon. Within these seemingly narrow limits the reader will find a wide variety of form and thought and feeling. It will be noticed that comparatively few of the pieces are among those in common use for public worship. No part of the editor's search has been so disappointing as that which led him among the hymn-books. It is well known that what may be called the singing qualities of a hymn are often in inverse ratio to the poetic. There are very many hymns, which, when removed from their setting, and analyzed as poems, are found to be commonplace, and barren of beauty. No piece, however, has been discarded from the collection simply because it was familiar, nor included simply because it was little known. Religious feeling and poetic beauty constitute the standard which the editor has sought to apply.

It is not claimed that the collection is complete, but that it is comprehensive and fairly representative. It contains one hundred and seventy-seven pieces, extending over fifteen centuries of sacred song, and representing the poets of eight distinct nationalities. It is hoped that the attempt made at classification and chronological arrangement will assist the reader in the ready use of the volume.

PREFATORY NOTE.

The notes prefixed to the hymns have been prepared with care from the best accessible sources. They are given in the belief that the interest of a hymn is enhanced by a knowledge of the circumstances in which it was written, or of the author. If inaccuracies exist, the editor will be glad to be informed of them, in order that they may be corrected in later editions.

The editor is indebted to Mr. Whittier, Bishop Coxe, Dr. Peabody, Mr. A. D. F. Randolph, Mr. C. B. Tillinghast, and Mr. A. P. Hitchcock, for encouragement or advice; and to A. D. F. Randolph & Co., Dr. Schaff, Houghton, Osgood & Co., Mrs. A. D. T. Whitney, Miss Emily Seaver, Miss Harriet McEwen Kimball, and Miss Emily P. Mann, for permission to use copyrighted poems.

Index of First Lines.

	PAGE
Again the Lord of life and light	211
Alas, poore death! where is thy glorie?	186
Alleluia! Alleluia!	66
Alleluia! Alleluia!	293
All hail! dear Conqueror! all hail!	263
All is o'er, — the pain, the sorrow	236
All praise to Him of Nazareth	316
Angels, roll the rock away	210
Angels, to our jubilee	94
A pathway opens from the tomb	306
Arise	247
Arise, my soul! awake from sleep	103
As spring's sweet breath after long wintry snow	291
As those who seek the break of day	18
Awake, glad soul! awake! awake!	261
Awake, thou wintry earth	301
Behold the day the Lord hath made	54
Blest morning, whose young dawning rays	201
Breezes of spring, all earth to life awaking	345
Calm they sit with closèd door	300
Christ has arisen	332
Christ hath arisen	141

INDEX OF FIRST LINES.

	PAGE
Christ hath arisen! O mountain peaks! attest!	233
Christ is become our Paschal Lamb	298
Christ is risen! Alleluia!	259
Christ is risen, the Lord is come	228
Christ the Lord is risen again	118
Christ the Lord is risen to-day	67
Christ the Lord is risen to-day	204
Christ, upon the Friday slain	56
Christ, we sing Thy saving passion	17
Christ with mighty triumph rises	91
Come, and let us drink of that new river	4
Come, ye faithful, raise the strain	12
Come, ye saints, look here and wonder	218
Dawn bursts o'er death's prison	163
Dawn of dawns, the Easter Day	339
Days grow longer, sunbeams stronger	308
Dear Saviour of a dying world	285
Death and darkness, get you packing!	199
Death, thou wast once an uncouth hideous thing	187
Done is a battle on the dragon black	169
Do saints keep holy day in heavenly places?	326
Ere yet the dawn has filled the skies	123
Eternal Father! at whose word	324
Fair spring, thou dearest season of the year	115
Far be sorrow, tears, and sighing	299
For Easter Day, O lilies white!	338
Forth to the Paschal Victim, Christians, bring	69
From death, Christ, on the Sabbath morn	105
Glory be to God on high	302
Hail, day of days! in peals of praise	36
Hail! day of joyous rest	245
Hail! the holy day of days	79
Hail the much-remembered day	52

INDEX OF FIRST LINES.

	PAGE
Hallelujah! Jesus lives!	139
Hallowed forever be that twilight hour.	329
He comes! He comes! the tomb,	282
He is risen! He is risen!	275
Helped by the Almighty's arm, at last.	87
Hence they have borne my Lord. Behold the stone	182
He's gone! see where His body lay	216
How brightly glows the morning red!	143
How shall we keep this holy day of gladness?	331
If the dark and awful tomb.	15
I have no wit, no words, no tears.	281
In the bonds of death He lay	120
In the tomb, behold, He lies	250
In Thy glorious resurrection	251
Into the dim earth's lowest parts descending.	7
I say to all men far and near	145
It is the noon of night.	277
Jesus Christ is risen to-day.	96
Jesus hath vanished; all in vain.	77
Jesus! in spices wrapped, and laid	264
Jesus lives: no longer now.	135
Jesus my Redeemer lives	127
Jesu, the very thought of Thee	45
Joy, O joy, ye broken-hearted!	64
Lamb, the once crucified	150
Let faithfull soules this double feast attend.	175
Let us rise in early morning.	6
Lift your glad voices in triumph on high	314
Light's glittering morn bedecks the sky	33
Lord, who createdst man in wealth and store	185
Lo! the day the Lord hath made.	224
Lo! the gates of death are broken	47
Mary to her Saviour's tomb.	207
Morning breaks upon the tomb	227

	PAGE
Morning of the Sabbath day	222
Most glorious Lord of lyfe that on this day	171
Now Morning lifts her dewy veil	83
Now the world's fresh dawn of birth	49
Now thy gentle Lamb, O Sion!	63
O Christians, let us joyful be!	106
O darkest woe!	125
O day of days! shall hearts set free	230
O glorious Head, Thou livest now	133
O mine eyes, be not so tearful	334
Once more thou comest, O delicious spring	317
On earth was darkness spread	335
O risen Lord, O conquering King	131
O Thou, the heavens' eternal King	85
O Thou who once from death didst rise	40
Our Paschal joy at last is here	161
Pain and toil are over now	276
Praise to Christ with suppliant voices	42
Purge we out the ancient leaven	59
Put on thy beautiful robes, Bride of Christ	296
Rejoice, dear Christendom, to-day	113
Rise again, yes, rise again, wilt thou	137
Rise, heart, thy Lord is risen : sing His praise	183
Rise, heir of fresh eternity	197
Sabbath of the saints of old	266
Saints on earth, and saints in light	74
Saviour of mankind, Man! Emmanuel!	172
Say, Earth, why hast thou got thee new attire?	177
See the land, her Easter keeping	274
Sing aloud, children	325
Sleep, sleep, old sun ; thou canst not have re-past	174
Smile praises, O sky!	81
So holy is this day of days	114

INDEX OF FIRST LINES. xiii

	PAGE
So rest, my rest	129
Spring is in its beauty glowing	70
Springtide birds are singing, singing	19
Stand on thy watch-tower, Habakkuk the seer	5
Still thy sorrow, Magdalena!	61
Sun, shine forth in all thy splendor	147
Tell us, Gard'ner, dost thou know	320
The calm of blessed night	257
The Church of God lifts up her voice	16
The foe behind, the deep before	271
The golden palace of my God	99
The graves grow thicker, and life's ways more bare	305
The happy morn is come	208
The Lord is risen indeed	220
The Lord of life is risen	154
The morning purples all the sky	38
The orient beams of Easter morn	88
There went three damsels at break of day	111
The setting orb of night her level ray	214
The supper of the Lamb to share	29
The tomb is empty: wouldst thou have it full?	254
The winter is over and gone at last	323
The world itself keeps Easter Day	343
They bound him well in the dungeon cell	288
They who with Mary came	14
This is the day the Lord hath made	180
This is the very day of God	27
Thou hallowed chosen morn of praise	10
Thou new Jerusalem, arise and shine!	11
Thou, that on the first of Easters	336
Thou whose sad heart and weeping head lyes low	200
Thou, who to save	90
'Tis He! 'tis He! I know him now	318
'Tis the day of resurrection	3
To Him who for our sins was slain	249
'Twas night! still night!	242

	PAGE
Up, and away	188
Up! sound your joyful songs victorious	156
Weeper! to thee how bright a morn was given	235
We keep the festival	31
Welcome, O day, in dazzling glory bright	313
Welcome the triumphal token	51
We were not with the faithful few	295
What faithless, froward, sinful man	190
What glorious light	196
What said He, Mary, unto thee?	268
Who comes? my soul, no longer doubt	213
Who deems the Saviour dead?	341
Who from the fiery furnace saved the three	8
Who is this that comes from Edom?	219
Why, thou never-setting Light	100
Words may not thy glory tell	75
Ye choirs of New Jerusalem	41
Ye sons and daughters of the King	72
Yes, the Redeemer rose	202

Index of Latin Hymns.

	PAGE
Ad cœnam Agni providi	29
Adeste, cœlitum chori	94
Ad regias Agni dapes	31
Ad templa nos rursus vocat	83
Alleluia! Alleluia! Finita jam sunt prœlia	66
A morte qui Te suscitans	40
Aurora cœlum purpurat	38
Aurora lucis dum novæ	88
Aurora lucis rutilat	33
Cedant justi signa luctus	64
Chorus Novæ Jerusalem	41
Cœli choris perennibus	74
Ecce dies celebris!	52
Ecce tempus est vernale	70
Erumpe tandem juste dolor	77
Forti tegente brachia	87
Hæc est dies triumphalis	51
Hæc est sancta solemnitas solemnitatum	79
Hic est dies verus Dei	27

xv

INDEX OF LATIN HYMNS.

	PAGE
Jesu, dulcis memoria	45
Jesu, Redemptor sæculi	90
Laudes Christo redempti voce	42
Mitis Agnus, Leo fortis	63
Mortis portis fractis, fortis	47
Mundi renovatio	49
O filii et filiæ	72
Plaudite cœli	81
Pone luctum, Magdalena!	61
Rex sempiterne cœlitum	85
Salve, dies dierum gloria	54
Salve, festa dies, toto venerabilis ævo	36
Sexta passus feria	56
Surgit Christus cum trophæo	91
Surrexit Christus hodie	96
Te quanta Victor funeris	75
Victimæ Paschali laudes	67, 69
Zyma vetus expurgetur	59

Index of Authors.

The names to which an asterisk is prefixed are those of authors concerning whom no biographical data have been obtained.

ADAM OF ST. VICTOR.	49, 51, 52, 54, 56, 59
ADAMS, SARAH FLOWER	247
ALEXANDER, CECIL FRANCES	275, 276
ALFORD, HENRY	257
ALLEN, WILLIAM	313
AMBROSE, ST.	27, 33
BARBAULD, ANNA LÆTITIA	211
BAYNES, ROBERT HALL	291
BEAUMONT, JOHN	175
BERNARD OF CLAIRVAUX	45
BETHUNE, GEORGE W.	318
*BLACKBURN, THOMAS	301
BOBROFF, SEMEN SERGEJEWITSCH	99, 100
BOEHMER, JUSTUS H.	131
BONAR, HORATIUS	254
BOWLES, WILLIAM LISLE	213
BRANDENBURG, ELECTRESS OF	127
BRYANT, WILLIAM CULLEN	316
CARY, PHŒBE	334
COLLYER, WILLIAM BENGO	227

INDEX OF AUTHORS.

COXE, A. CLEVELAND	320, 323
CRASHAW, RICHARD	197
CROSWELL, WILLIAM	317
DIX, WILLIAM CHATTERTON	296
DODDRIDGE, PHILIP	202
DONNE, JOHN	174
DUNBAR, WILLIAM	169
FABER, FREDERICK W.	263, 264
FLETCHER, GILES	177
FORTUNATUS, VENANTIUS	36
FRANK, SOLOMON	129
FRANZEN, F. MICHAEL	163
FULBERT OF CHARTRES	41
GARVE, CHRISTIAN	139
GELLERT, CHRISTIAN F.	135
GOETHE, JOHANN WOLFGANG VON	141
GRAHAME, JAMES	214
GREENWELL, DORA	268
GRUNDTVIG, NICOLAI FREDERIK SEVERIN	105
HARDENBERG, FRIEDRICH VON	145
HARVEY, CHRISTOPHER	188
HAWEIS, THOMAS	208
HEERMAN, JOHANN	123
HEMANS, FELICIA	233, 235
HERBERT, GEORGE	183, 185, 186, 187
HERRICK, ROBERT	182
HILL, THOMAS	324
INGELOW, JEAN	277
JANVIER, FRANCIS DE HAES	341
JOHN OF DAMASCUS	3, 4, 5, 6, 7, 8, 10, 11, 12, 14, 15
KEBLE, JOHN	230
KELLY, THOMAS	216, 218, 219, 220

KIMBALL, HARRIET M.	338, 339
KINGO, THOMAS	103
KINGSLEY, CHARLES	274
KLOPSTOCK, FRIEDRICH G.	137
LANGE, JOHANN PETER	154
LITTLEDALE, RICHARD F.	288
LOWE, MARTHA P.	329
LUTHER, MARTIN	120
MANT, RICHARD	224
MILMAN, HENRY H.	228
MONSELL, JOHN S. B.	259, 261
MONTGOMERY, JAMES	222
MOULTRIE, GERARD	282
MOULTRIE, JOHN	236
NEALE, JOHN MASON	271
NEWMAN, JOHN HENRY	242
NEWTON, JOHN	207
NOVALIS. — See HARDENBERG.	
PETER THE VENERABLE	47
PETERSEN, LAURENCE	161
QUEINFURT, CONRAD VON	115
* RAMUS, ——	106
RIST, JOHANN VON	125
ROSSETTI, CHRISTINA G.	281
RUSSELL, ARTHUR T.	249, 250
SANDYS, GEORGE	172
SCHWEIZER, META HAUSSER	150
SEAVER, EMILY	331
SCOTT, THOMAS	210
SPENSER, EDMUND	171
SPITTA, C. J. P.	147

TAYLOR, JEREMY	196
TERSTEEGEN, GERHARD	133
THOMPSON, ALEXANDER RAMSAY	325
TREND, HENRY	245
TOURNEAUX, NICHOLAS LE	94
VAUGHN, HENRY	199, 200
WARE, HENRY, Jun.	314
WARING, ANNA LÆTITIA	285
WASHBURN, E. A.	332
WATTS, ISAAC	201
WESLEY, CHARLES	204
WHITNEY, A. D. T.	326
WHYTEHEAD, THOMAS	266
WITHER, GEORGE	180
WORDSWORTH, CHRISTOPHER	251

Index of Translators.

BLEW, WILLIAM JOHN .	94
BORTHWICK, JANE	139
BOWRING, JOHN .	99, 100
CASWALL, EDWARD .	45, 69, 77, 85
CHAMBERS, JOHN DAVID .	87, 88
CHANDLER, JOHN .	83
CHARLES, ELIZABETH .	27, 29, 47, 81
COX, FRANCES ELIZABETH	135
DIX, WILLIAM CHATTERTON	14, 15, 16, 17, 18
FINDLATER, Mrs. ERIC	139
HARBAUGH, HENRY .	154
HEDGE, FREDERICK H.	141
HEWETT, JOHN WILLIAM .	79, 91
HITCHCOCK, A. P.	163
KYNASTON, HERBERT .	64
LITTLEDALE, RICHARD FREDERICK	42, 56, 143, 161
MASSIE, RICHARD	147
NEALE, JOHN MASON,	3, 4, 5, 6, 7, 8, 10, 11, 12, 33, 52, 59, 66, 72

INDEX OF TRANSLATORS.

Onslow, Phipps	19, 74
Porter, Thomas C.	150
Smith, John George	40
Tait, Gilbert	103, 105, 106
Thompson, Alexander Ramsay	31, 38
Thompson, Henry	156
Trend, Henry	63, 70
Washburn, E. A.	61
Weiss, Michael	118
Williams, Isaac	90
Winkworth, Catherine	111, 113, 114, 115, 118, 120, 123, 125, 127, 131, 133, 137, 145
Worsley, P. S.	49, 51

Introduction.

IN the early Church, the Resurrection of Christ was regarded as the most important fact in the record of His life, and still more as the foremost article of Christian belief, — as that without which it was impossible to place any confidence in the Saviour's teachings, or to ascribe any efficacy to His death. "If Christ be not risen," writes St. Paul, "our preaching is vain, and your faith is also vain." This event has left a deeper impress on the world's history than any other on record. It does not depend for its evidence even on the Gospels. Were they lost or discredited, there yet occurred, beyond a doubt, in the century to which they relate, intellectual, moral, and social developments and changes, which can be accounted for only by the resurrection of Jesus from the dead. The sceptics of our own time admit that the Apostles could not have held together or pursued their work of propagandism, and that Christianity could not have survived its Founder's cross, had not His followers felt certain that their Master had risen, and that they had seen Him. It is conceded even by Renan, that the stories of the Evangelists are honest statements of what they thought had passed under the eyes of various groups of disciples, — at one time, of several hundred persons. But he does not explain how an optical illusion could have been kept up at intervals for forty days, before different groups, and in clear sunlight, in the open air, on the lake-shore and the mountain-side, no less than in the evening-gloom of the upper chamber.

That the whole Church believed in the reality of this life from the dead, we have abundant evidence. St. Paul's earliest Epistles were confessedly written but a few years after the crucifixion, and they constantly refer to the Resurrection as a fact undoubted in Christian circles. In the generation next succeeding that of the Apostles, there grew up a controversy as to the proper time of keeping Easter; and appeal was then made to primitive usage, as if the Resurrection had been celebrated from the very first. Indeed, we know it had from the beginning a weekly celebration: for there is not the slightest trace of any religious observance of the first day of the week before the time of Christ; while we find that it was a day of Christian worship within a few weeks after He had disappeared from the earth, and we have abundant proof that it was so hallowed as the day on which He rose.

This event is properly called the *resurrection*, the *rising again*, — not the coming of the dead to life, but the re-appearance of Him who had lived on in death, and who returned to the dead body to show that it is the body alone that can die. Thus our Saviour in His own person " abolished death," — blotted it out from among the possible experiences of any and every living soul. Those, then, who have gone from us, and have seemed to die, still live ; and for us death will be but a passage from life to life.

All this might, indeed, have been proclaimed on Divine authority; but mere words — even though words of God — would have failed fully to meet man's needs. No event takes so strong hold as death on the imagination and the emotional nature. The altered countenance, the wasted frame, the agony of parting, the grave with its mysterious horrors, cannot but recur to make the memory of the departed intensely painful, and to shroud in the densest gloom the prospect of our own dissolution. It is therefore a solace of indispensable need, and unspeakable worth and efficacy, that all the sad accessories of death in their most appalling forms were about our Lord, and that they have all been transfigured by His rising, — symbols no longer of decay and corruption, but of emancipation into the higher and eternal life.

The Resurrection is thus brought within the field of poetry. While it commends itself to faith by an array of impregnable proof, it equally appeals to feeling and sentiment. The gorgeous beauty of an Oriental spring surrounding the Sepulchre with bloom and fragrance; the rolling-away of the rock by unseen hands; the white-robed angels where the dead had lain; the procession of the sorrowing women; the interview with Mary Magdalene; the movements — so perfectly in character — of Peter and John; the walk to Emmaus, and the supper there; the leaping from mouth to mouth and from heart to heart of the glad tidings, "The Lord has risen indeed!" — these, and not a few other features of the scene and incidents of the day, have in them elements of transcending beauty and grandeur, and furnish a mine of poetic fancy and imagery, which has been worked from the very birth-time of Christian hymnology, and which will still open new and rich veins for sacred lyrics in all coming generations.

A volume of Easter-hymns might, at first thought, promise but little variety. The truth is far otherwise. As from a few lines and tints an endless number of patterns, all differing from one another, may be drawn for a carpet or a wall-paper, so may innumerable combinations and groupings be made from a few simple incidents, with the associations inseparable from them, and the thoughts that naturally flow from them. It is thus that no two hymns on the same subject are alike, and that no hymn that unites devotional and poetic merit can ever be dispensed with because of its resemblance to another. This is especially true of the hymns and poems that commemorate the Resurrection. No theme of sacred song has a wider range. It connects itself with all our sorrows, our hopes, and our joys; with all that sheds sun-rays of heaven upon our earthly life; with the blessed memories of those who sleep in Jesus; with the fellowship that unites the households which death has parted, and makes of the whole family of Christian believers " one church, above, beneath."

Nor has there been any subject which has called forth so wide a diversity of inspiration. We have the rich mellifluous strains of the old Greek hymns, the terse, sonorous, majestic melodies of the Latin Church, the calm, meditative fervor of the German Muse, and, in our own tongue, the quaintness of our early poets, and, in later time, every mood of lyric rhythm, now slow and solemn, now soaring and jubilant as the song of the lark, and again in a tone of tender and subdued gladness, as of one whose inward vision turns from the grave of buried kindred to the place where the Lord lay.

May this Easter offering lift many hearts in glad thanksgiving to Him who has conquered death, in whom the dead live, and in whom he that believeth shall never die!

ANDREW P. PEABODY.

"STILL on the lips of all we question
  The finger of God's silence lies:
Shall the lost hands in ours be folded?
  Will the shut eyelids ever rise?

O friends! no proof beyond this yearning,
  This outreach of our souls, we need:
God will not mock the hope He giveth;
  No love He prompts shall vainly plead.

Then let us stretch our hands in darkness,
  And call our loved ones o'er and o'er:
Some time their arms shall close about us,
  And the old voices speak once more."

J. G. WHITTIER.

From the Greek.

Resurgit.

'Tis the Day of Resurrection.

By St. John Damascene, who was unquestionably the greatest of the poets of the Eastern Church. The date of his birth is unknown; and of his death all that is certain is that it occurred after 754, and before 787. He was born of a good family, made great progress in philosophy, was an eloquent adversary of the Iconoclasts, resided for a time at the monastery of St. Sabas in Palestine, and late in life was ordained priest of the Church of Jerusalem. The following is the first Ode of his great Easter Canon, which is to this day sung by the Greek Church, at the first hour of Easter morning, with every sort of jubilant accompaniment, — the flashing of light from thousands of tapers, the joyous strains of bands of music, the roll of drums, and thunder of cannon. The translation is by Rev. J. M. Neale, D.D., and is contained in his "Hymns of the Eastern Church." See biographical note prefixed to the piece, "The Foe behind, the Deep before."

'TIS the Day of Resurrection:
    Earth! tell it out abroad!
  The Passover of Gladness,
    The Passover of God.
From Death to Life eternal,
  From this world to the sky,
Our Christ hath brought us over,
  With hymns of victory.

Our hearts be pure from evil,
  That we may see aright
The Lord in rays eternal
  Of Resurrection-Light;
And, listening to His accents,
  May hear, so calm and plain,
His own *All Hail!* — and, hearing,
  May raise the victor strain!

Now let the Heavens be joyful!
  Let Earth her song begin!
Let the round world keep triumph,
  And all that is therein;
Invisible and visible,
  Their notes let all things blend;
For Christ the Lord hath risen, —
  Our joy that hath no end.

Come, and Let us Drink of that New River.

By St. John Damascene: the third Ode in his Easter Canon. Translated by Dr. Neale.

COME, and let us drink of that New River,
  Not from barren rock divinely poured,

But the Fount of Life that is forever
  From the sepulchre of Christ the Lord.

All the world hath bright illumination, —
  Heaven and Earth, and things beneath the earth:
'Tis the festival of all Creation;
  Christ hath risen, Who gave Creation birth.

Yesterday with Thee in burial lying,
  Now to-day with Thee arisen, I rise:
Yesterday the partner of Thy dying,
  With Thyself upraise me to the skies.

Stand on thy Watch-Tower, Habakkuk the Seer.

By St. John Damascene: the fourth Ode in his Easter Canon. Translated by Dr. Neale.

STAND on thy watch-tower, Habakkuk the Seer,
  And show the Angel, radiant in his light:
"To-day," saith he, "Salvation shall appear,
  Because the Lord hath risen as God of might."

The male that opes the Virgin's womb is He:
  The Lamb of Whom His faithful people eat;
Our truer Passover, from blemish free;
  Our very God, Whose name is all complete.

This yearling Lamb, our Sacrifice most blest,
  Our glorious Crown, for all men freely dies:
Behold our Pascha, beauteous from His rest,
  The healing Sun of Righteousness arise.

Before the ark, a type to pass away,
  David of old time danced: we, holier race,
Seeing the Antitype come forth to-day,
  Hail, with a shout, Christ's own almighty grace.

Let us Rise in Early Morning.

By St. John Damascene: the fifth Ode in his Easter Canon. Translated by Dr. Neale.

LET us rise in early morning,
    And, instead of ointments, bring
  Hymns of praises to our Master,
    And His Resurrection sing:
We shall see the Sun of Justice,
  Risen with healing on His wing.

Thy unbounded loving-kindness,
 They that groaned in Hades' chain,
Prisoners, from afar beholding,
 Hastened to the light again;
And to that eternal Pascha
 Wove the dance, and raised the strain.

Go ye forth, His Saints, to meet Him!
 Go with lamps in every hand!
From the sepulchre He riseth:
 Ready for the Bridegroom stand:
And the Pascha of Salvation
 Hail, with his triumphant band!

Into the Dim Earth's Lowest Parts Descending.

By St. John Damascene: the sixth Ode in his Easter Canon. Translated by Dr. Neale.

INTO the dim earth's lowest parts descending,
 And bursting by Thy might the infernal chain
That bound the prisoners, Thou, at three days' ending,
 As Jonah from the whale, hast risen again.

Thou brakest not the seal, Thy surety's
    token,
  Arising from the tomb, Who left'st in birth
The portals of virginity unbroken,
    Opening the gates of heaven to sons of
    earth.

Thou, Sacrifice ineffable and living,
  Didst to the Father by Thyself atone
As God eternal; resurrection giving
  To Adam, general parent, by Thine own.

Who from the Fiery Furnace Saved the Three.

By St. John Damascene: the seventh Ode of his Easter Canon. Translated by Dr. Neale.

WHO from the fiery furnace saved the
    Three,
  Suffers as mortal; that, His Passion
    o'er,
This mortal, triumphing o'er death, might be
  Vested with immortality once more:
    He whom our fathers still confest
    God over all, forever blest.

The women with their ointment seek the
    tomb;
  And Whom they mourned as dead, with
    many a tear,
They worship now, joy dawning on their
    gloom,
  As Living God, as mystic Passover;
    Then to the Lord's disciples gave
    The tidings of the vanquished grave.

We keep the festal of the death of death;
  Of hell o'erthrown; the first-fruits, pure
    and bright,
Of life eternal; and, with joyous breath,
  Praise Him that won the victory by His
    might:
    Him Whom our fathers still confest
    God over all, forever blest.

All hallowed festival, in splendor born!
  Night of salvation and of glory! Night
Fore-heralding the Resurrection morn!
  When from the tomb the everlasting Light,
    A glorious frame once more His own,
    Upon the world in splendor shone.

Thou Hallowed Chosen Morn of Praise.

By St. John Damascene: the eighth Ode of his Easter Canon. Translated by Dr. Neale.

THOU hallowed chosen morn of praise,
    That best and greatest shinest!
Lady and Queen and Day of days,
    Of things divine, divinest!
      On thee our praises Christ adore
      For ever and for evermore.

Come, let us taste the Vine's new fruit,
    For heavenly joy preparing;
To-day the branches with the Root
    In Resurrection sharing:
      Whom as True God our hymns adore,
      For ever and for evermore.

Rise, Sion, rise, and, looking forth,
    Behold thy children round thee!
From East and West, and South and North,
    Thy scattered sons have found thee!
      And in thy bosom Christ adore
      For ever and for evermore.

O Father! O co-equal Son!
　O co-eternal Spirit!
In Persons Three, in Substance One,
　And One in power and merit:
　　In Thee baptized, we Thee adore
　　For ever and for evermore!

Thou New Jerusalem, Arise and Shine!

By St. John Damascene: the ninth Ode in his Easter Canon. Translated by Dr. Neale. There is another translation by William Chatterton Dix, beginning, " Shine, shine, O New Jerusalem!"

THOU New Jerusalem, arise and shine!
　The glory of the Lord on thee hath risen.
Sion, exult! rejoice with joy divine!
　Mother of God! Thy Son hath burst his prison!

O heavenly Voice! O word of purest love!
　" Lo! I am with you alway to the end!"
This is the anchor, steadfast from above,—
　The golden anchor, whence our hopes depend.

O Christ, our Pascha! greatest, holiest, best!
  God's Word and Wisdom and effectual
      Might!
Thy fuller, lovelier presence manifest,
  In that eternal realm that knows no night!

Come, Ye Faithful, Raise the Strain.

From St. John Damascene, by Dr. Neale. It is commonly classed among Easter hymns, although it belongs in his canon for St. Thomas's Sunday, or Low Sunday, as indicated by the allusion in the last stanza.

COME, ye faithful, raise the strain
    Of triumphant gladness!
  God hath brought His Israel
    Into joy from sadness;
  Loosed from Pharaoh's bitter yoke
    Jacob's sons and daughters;
  Led them with unmoistened foot
    Through the Red Sea waters.

'Tis the spring of souls to-day!
    Christ hath burst His prison;
  And, from three days' sleep in death,
    As a sun hath risen.

All the winter of our sins,
   Long and dark, is flying
From His light, to Whom we give
   Laud and praise undying.

Now the queen of seasons, bright
   With the day of splendor,
With the royal Feast of feasts,
   Comes its joy to render;
Comes to glad Jerusalem,
   Who with true affection
Welcomes, in unwearied strains,
   Jesu's Resurrection.

Neither might the gates of death,
   Nor the tomb's dark portal,
Nor the watchers, nor the seal,
   Hold Thee as a mortal;
But to-day amidst the twelve
   Thou didst stand, bestowing
That Thy peace, which evermore
   Passeth human knowing.

They who with Mary came.

From the Greek of St. John Damascene, translated by William Chatterton Dix. See biographical note prefixed to the hymn, "Put on Thy Beautiful Robes, Bride of Christ."

THEY who with Mary came,
   Before the dawn of day,
  Soon found that from the sepulchre
   The stone was rolled away.

Then to those fearful souls
   The shining Angel said,—
Him who in light eternal dwells,
   Why seek ye with the dead?

The grave-clothes see, and haste
   The joyful news to tell:
The Lord is risen, and He hath been
   The death of death and hell.

He is the Son of God,
   Who saves the human race:
No more shall death destroy, no more
   The ancient foe have place.

If the Dark and Awful Tomb.

This also is from the Greek of St. John Damascene, and the translation by William C. Dix.

IF the dark and awful tomb
  Thou, immortal One, hast known,
 Rising, in Thy deathless bloom,
  Hades Thou hast overthrown.

Yes; as Victor Thou hast burst
  All the bands of hell, and said,
Hail! to those who sought Thee first,
  Bearing ointment for the dead;

Peace, Thy earliest, sweetest gift,
  Unto Thine Apostles given;
All the fallen Thou didst lift
  From the gates of hell to heaven.

The Church of God Lifts up Her Voice.

A Greek Paschal hymn, from the Offices of the Greek Church, translated by WILLIAM C. DIX.

HE Church of God lifts up her voice;
To-day both heaven and earth rejoice:
The gladsome Passover is here, —
The Passover of Christ most dear.

The Passover that frees from woe,
That binds in chains the ancient foe,
That opens wide the heavenly gate,
The Lord's own day, we celebrate.

From "very early" until night,
One strain we lift, one shout of might:
With Eucharist the morn arose,
With Hallelujahs day shall close.

O Christ, eternal Pascha, Thou,
And Crown for every willing brow!
Thou spotless Lamb and Victor bright,
Arrayed in more than morning light!

On this Thy Resurrection-day
Be strife and hate put far away,
That those who in thy likeness live
May each his brother's wrongs forgive.

The earth in festal raiment stands,
The floods for gladness clap their hands:
Then higher still, and higher raise
The true, the living Pascha's praise.

Christ, we sing Thy Saving Passion.

From the Offices of the Greek Church, translated by WILLIAM C. DIX.

CHRIST, we sing Thy saving passion;
   Thine arising glorify:
Death forever to abolish,
   Thou upon the Cross didst die;
Then from Hades Thou didst hasten,
   As alone omnipotent:
Grant us peace in life, Redeemer,
   Joy when earthly life is spent.

Sing we now Thy condescension,
   Christ, with God the Father One;
We in lofty hymns will praise Thee,
   Mary-Mother's Blessed Son.

Thou for us as Man didst suffer,
　　Willingly the Cross didst bear;
That Thy resurrection-glory,
　　We, the sons of men, may share.

Coming as from bridal chamber,
　　Robed with orient morning-light;
Bringing to the world salvation,
　　Spoiling hell of all her might;
Raising, by Thy resurrection,
　　Man to dignity most high:
Christ, may we with pure thanksgiving
　　Thee forever glorify!

As Those who Seek the Break of Day.

Translated from the Offices of the Greek Church, by WILLIAM C. DIX.

AS those who seek the break of day
　　Full early in the morning,
　The women came where Jesus lay,
　　Who late had borne the scorning.
Sweet ointment in their hands they brought,
　　And, ere the sun had risen,
The Sun of Righteousness they sought,
　　Now set within death's prison.

And thus they cried: "The Body here,
  Let us give new anointing;
The quickening flesh, the Body dear,
  Which, by Divine appointing,
From this dark sepulchre shall rise,
  And Adam's race deliver,
And lift the fallen to the skies,
  To reign in bliss forever."

And, like the Magi, hasten we
  To Him with love adoring:
Sweet spices, too, our gifts shall be,
  And we must weep, imploring
That He, in swaddling clothes no more,
  But in fine linen lying,
Would grant the fallen, when life is o'er,
  The gift of life undying.

Springtide Birds are Singing, Singing.

The following is contained in "Lyra Mystica," under the title "The Salutation of the Greek Church on Easter Day." The translation is by Rev. PHIPPS ONSLOW. See the biographical notice prefixed to the hymn, "Saints on Earth, and Saints in Light."

SPRINGTIDE birds are singing, sing-
    ing,
  For the daybreak in the East:
Silver bells are ringing, ringing,
  For the Church's glorious Feast.

Christ is risen! Christ is risen!
  Sin's long triumph now is o'er.
Christ is risen! Death's dark prison
  Now can hold His Saints no more.
    Christ is risen! risen, Brother!
    Brother, Christ is risen indeed!

Holy women sought Him weeping,
  Weeping at the break of dawn, —
Sought their Lord where He lay sleeping,
  In the love of hearts forlorn.
Life for death on death's throne meeting,
  Joy for sorrow, faith for fear,
For their tears the Angel's greeting, —
  Christ is risen! He is not here.
    Christ is risen! risen, Brother!
    Brother, Christ is risen indeed!

Loved Apostles, scarce believing
  In His triumph o'er the grave,
Hear the tale amid their grieving,
  Hasten eager to the Cave;
Find the folded grave-clothes lying,
  Death's unloosed and shattered chain,
Find Him gone, death's power defying,
  From the Cavern sealed in vain.
    Christ is risen! risen, Brother!
    Brother, Christ is risen indeed!

Mary comes, a refuge seeking
  For her mourning and her shame:
Lo! a well-known voice is speaking;
  Lo! the Master calls her name.
First, the life o'er sin victorious,
  She who wept for sin adored,
For her tears the mission glorious
  To announce the Risen Lord.
    Christ is risen! risen, Brother!
    Brother, Christ is risen indeed!

For her tears, O glad reversing
  Of the Woman's work of old,
Glorious tidings now rehearsing;
  For the tale in Eden told,
Woman's voice, that tale supplying,
  Brought in death by Satan's lie:
Woman's voice is now replying, —
  Christ is risen! we shall not die.
    Christ is risen! risen, Brother!
    Brother, Christ is risen indeed!

Where the noontide rays are falling
  On the rugged mountain-side,
Brethren journey, sad recalling
  How He loved, and how He died.

He is with them! He is hearing
   How their trust and hope had fled,
To their loving faith appearing
   In the blessing of the Bread.
        Christ is risen! risen, Brother!
        Brother, Christ is risen indeed!

Flashing back the sunset glory,
   Burns a casement high and dim:
There the Ten, on all His Story
   Sadly dwelling, speak of Him.
He is there! the Light that never
   Into twilight fades away;
Day-star of the Dawn that ever
   Breaks into the perfect Day!
        Christ is risen! risen, Brother!
        Brother, Christ is risen indeed!

Saints, your Cross in patience bearing,
   Mourners stained with many a tear,
Penitents, in sorrow wearing
   Darkest weeds of shame and fear,—
Christ is risen! lose your sadness,
   Joying with the joyous throng:
Faithful hearts will find their gladness,
   Joining in the Easter song,
        Christ is risen! risen, Brother!
        Brother, Christ is risen indeed!

Christ is risen! Christ the Living,
　All His mourners' tears to stay;
Christ is risen! Christ, forgiving,
　Wipes the stain of sin away.
Christ is risen! Christ is risen!
　Sin's long triumph now is o'er;
Christ is risen! Death's dark prison
　Holds His faithful never more.
　　　Christ is risen! risen, Brother!
　　　Brother, Christ is risen indeed!

From the Latin.

This is the Very Day of God.

(Hic est Dies verus Dei.)

By St. Ambrose, born probably at Treves, about 340, died in 397. His father was prefect of Gaul, and the son was intended for a secular career. He practised as an advocate at Milan, and was far advanced in civil preferment — having been appointed consular prefect of Liguria in 370 — when he was suddenly chosen Bishop of Milan, in 374, by an impulsive and unanimous vote of the people, although he was then only a layman, and unbaptized. He was a man of dauntless courage, and his strong and austere hymns inspired the people to render him their support in his defence of the integrity of the Creed, and the spiritual authority of the Church. Many hymns have been ascribed to him on insufficient evidence: the authenticity of the following rests on the excellent authority of F. J. Mone. The translation is by Mrs. Elizabeth Charles.

THIS is the very day of God:
Serene with holy light it came, —
In which the stream of sacred blood
Swept over the world's crime and shame.

Lost souls with faith once more it filled,
The darkness from blind eyes dissolved:
Whose load of fear too great to yield,
Seeing the dying thief absolved?

Changing the cross for the reward,
That moment's faith obtains his Lord:
Before the just his spirit flies;
The first-fruits enters Paradise.

The angels ponder, wondering;
They see the body's pain and strife,
They see to Christ the guilty cling,
And reap at once the blessed life.

O admirable Mystery!
The sins of all are laid on Thee;
And Thou, to cleanse the world's deep stain,
As man dost bear the sins of men.

What can be ever more sublime?
That grace might meet the guilt of time,
Love doth the bonds of fear undo,
And death restores our life anew.

Death's fatal spear himself doth wound;
With his own fetters he is bound.
Lo! dead the Life of all men lies,
That life anew for all might rise.

That, since death thus hath passed on all,
The dead might all arise again;
By his own death-blow death might fall,
And o'er his unshared fall complain.

𝕿𝖍𝖊 𝕾𝖚𝖕𝖕𝖊𝖗 𝖔𝖋 𝖙𝖍𝖊 𝕷𝖆𝖒𝖇 𝖙𝖔 𝕾𝖍𝖆𝖗𝖊.

(Ad Cænam Agni providi.)

An old Paschal Hymn, probably sung in the early Church by the newly-baptized catechumens, when, clad in white, they for the first time approached the Lord's table. Translated by Mrs. CHARLES. Dr. Neale's version begins, "The Lamb's high banquet we await." The date of the hymn is uncertain; but it is one of the most ancient, and has been by some ascribed to St. Ambrose.

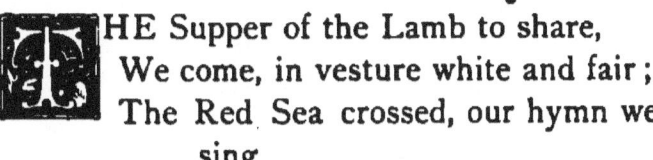HE Supper of the Lamb to share,
We come, in vesture white and fair;
The Red Sea crossed, our hymn we sing
To Christ, our Captain and our King.

His holy body on the cross,
Parched, on that altar hung for us;
And, drinking of His crimson blood,
We live upon the living God.

Protected in the Paschal night
From the destroying angel's might,
And by a powerful hand set free
From Pharaoh's bitter slavery.

For Christ our Passover is slain,
The Lamb is offered not in vain;

With truth's sincere unleavened bread,
His flesh He gave, His blood He shed.

O Victim! worthy Thou forever,
Who didst the bands of hell dissever!
Redeem Thy captives from the foe,
The gift of life afresh bestow.

When Christ from out the tomb arose,
Victor o'er hell and all His foes,
The tyrant forth in chains He drew,
And planted Paradise anew.

Author of all, to Thee we pray,
In this our Easter joy to-day:
From every weapon Death can wield,
Thy trusting people ever shield!

We Keep the Festival.

(Ad regias Agni dapes.)

From the Roman Breviary, altered from the preceding Paschal Hymn, "Ad Cœnam Agni providi." The following translation is by Rev. Dr. ALEXANDER RAMSAY THOMPSON of New York, and was contributed to Dr. Schaff's "Christ in Song." Dr. Thompson was born in New York, 1822; graduated at the University of New York, 1842; and was ordained minister of the Dutch Reformed Church. He served for some years as colleague of the late Rev. Dr. Bethune. Another version, by Edward Caswall, begins, "Now at the Lamb's high royal feast." The spirited version in the Episcopal Hymnal, beginning, "At the Lamb's high feast we sing," is largely altered by the compilers of "Hymns Ancient and Modern," from a translation by Robert Campbell (1850). The hymn beginning, "Once the angel started back," in the Episcopal Hymnal, is a part of a translation of the same hymn, by JOHN WILLIAMS (born at Deerfield, Mass., in 1817; Assistant Bishop of Connecticut, 1851-1865; Bishop, 1865 to the present time).

WE keep the festival
  Of the slain Lamb our King;
  The Red Sea passed,
  And safe at last,
Our Leader's praise we sing.

His love ineffable
He pledged in precious blood;
  And Priest most high,
  The altar by,
Himself devoting, stood.

The sacred crimson sign
The avenging angel knew;
   And the sea fled
   Back at Christ's tread,
And gave a pathway through.

Christ is our Passover!
And we will keep the feast
   With the new leaven,
   The bread of Heaven:
All welcome, even the least!

O Heavenly Champion!
Death thought to vanquish Thee!
   But Death is slain;
   And Thou again
Art risen, and we are free.

Hail, mighty Conqueror!
Under Thy glorious feet
   The tyrant lies,
   And gasps, and dies:
What praise for Thee is meet?

Forth from the gloomy prison
Jesus, we follow Thee,
   With broken chain,
   With ended pain,
To life and liberty!

All glory be to Thee!
All worship to Thy name!
Thee we adore,
And evermore
Will celebrate thy fame!

Light's Glittering Morn Bedecks the Sky.

(Aurora lucis rutilat.)

Ascribed to St. AMBROSE, 340-397. The following version is given by the compilers of "Hymns Ancient and Modern," altered from Dr. Neale's translation. Mrs. Charles has written a somewhat smoother and freer translation; but the following is preferable, because of its close adherence to the form and spirit of the original. Mrs. Charles's version begins, "The morning kindles all the sky."

LIGHT'S glittering morn bedecks the sky,
Heaven thunders forth its victor-cry,
The glad earth shouts her triumph high,
And groaning hell makes wild reply;

While He, the King, the mighty King,
Despoiling Death of all its sting,
And trampling down the powers of night,
Brings forth His ransomed saints to Light.

His Tomb of late the threefold guard
Of watch and stone and seal had barred;
But now, in pomp and triumph high,
He comes from death to Victory.

The pains of hell are loosed at last,
The days of mourning now are past;
An Angel robed in light hath said,
"The Lord is risen from the dead."

The Apostles' hearts were full of pain
For their dear Lord so lately slain,
By rebel servants doomed to die
A death of cruel agony.

With gentle voice the Angel gave
The women tidings at the grave:
"Fear not, your Master shall ye see;
He goes before to Galilee."

Then, hastening on their eager way
The joyful tidings to convey,
Their Lord they met, their living Lord,
And, falling at His feet, adored.

The Eleven, when they hear, with speed
To Galilee forthwith proceed,

That there once more they may behold
The Lord's dear Face, as He foretold.

That Easter-tide with joy was bright,
The sun shone out with fairer light,
When, to their longing eyes restored,
The Apostles saw their risen Lord.

He bade them see His hands, His side,
Where yet the glorious wounds abide;
O tokens true, which made it plain
Their Lord indeed was risen again!

Jesu, the King of Gentleness,
Do Thou Thyself our hearts possess,
That we may give Thee, all our days,
The tribute of our grateful praise!

Hail, Day of Days! In Peals of Praise.

(Salve, festa Dies, toto venerabilis ævo.)

By VENANTIUS FORTUNATUS, Bishop of Poictiers, born in 530, died in 609. His poems are the connecting link between those of Sedulius and Prudentius and those of the middle ages. He was long the fashionable poet of his day; but later in life his aspirations and his verse took on a holier character, and he wrote some beautiful hymns. The following translation by W. J. C. is a very free one, in a different measure from that of the original. There is another English version by Mrs. Charles; also another by the translator of the following, identical as to the first stanza, but differing widely as to the others.

HAIL, Day of days! in peals of praise
    Throughout all ages owned,
When Christ, our God, hell's empire trod,
    And high o'er heaven was throned.

This glorious morn the world new-born
    In rising beauty shows:
How, with her Lord to life restored,
    Her gifts and graces rose!

The spring serene in sparkling sheen
    The flower-clad earth arrays:
Heaven's portal bright its radiant light
    In fuller flood displays.

The fiery sun in loftier noon
　　O'er heaven's high orbit shines,
As o'er the tide of waters wide
　　He rises and declines.

From hell's deep gloom, from earth's dark
　　　　tomb,
　　The Lord in triumph soars:
The forests raise their leafy praise,
　　The flowery field adores.

As star by star He mounts afar,
　　And hell imprisoned lies,
Let stars and light and depth and height
　　In Hallelujahs rise.

Lo! He Who died, the Crucified,
　　God over all He reigns;
On Him we call, His creatures all,
　　Who heaven and earth sustains.

The Morning Purples all the Sky.

(Aurora cælum purpurat.)

An ancient Paschal Hymn, found in manuscripts at least as old as the beginning of the ninth century. There are several different texts in the original. The translation which follows is by Rev. Dr. A. R. Thompson of New York, and was contributed to Dr. Schaff's "Christ in Song." There are other translations, by Rev. J. Chandler, "This Holy Morn, so fair and bright;" and by Caswall, "The Dawn was purpling over the Sky."

THE morning purples all the sky,
    The air with praises rings;
Defeated hell stands sullen by,
    The world exulting sings;
Glory to God! our glad lips cry:
    All praise and worship be
On earth, in heaven, to God Most High,
    For Christ's great victory!

While He, the King all strong to save,
    Rends the dark doors away,
And through the breaches of the grave
    Strides forth into the day,
Glory to God! our glad lips cry:
    All praise and worship be
On earth, in heaven, to God Most High,
    For Christ's great victory!

Death's captive, in his gloomy prison
   Fast fettered He has lain;
But he has mastered Death, has risen,
   And Death wears now the chain.
Glory to God! our glad lips cry:
   All praise and worship be
On earth, in heaven, to God Most High,
   For Christ's great victory!

The shining angels cry, "Away
   With grief! no spices bring;
Not tears, but songs, this joyful day,
   Should greet the rising King!"
Glory to God! our glad lips cry:
   All praise and worship be
On earth, in heaven, to God Most High,
   For Christ's great victory!

That Thou our Paschal Lamb mayst be,
   And endless joy begin,
Jesus, Deliverer, set us free
   From the dread death of sin.
Glory to God! our glad lips cry:
   All praise and worship be
On earth, in heaven, to God Most High,
   For Christ's great victory!

O Thou Who once from Death didst Rise.

(A morte qui Te suscitans.)

An ancient Compline hymn, translated by JOHN GEORGE SMITH.

O THOU Who once from death didst rise,
Effulgent with new victories,
Lighten the darkness of our night,
And shield us with Thy gifts of might.

Oh, grant that when our limbs shall lie
Wrapt in sleep's needful lethargy,
Our spirits then, from fetters free,
May upward soar, O Lord, to Thee.

And, lest the fiery darts that fly
By night should work us injury,
With Thy right hand victorious keep
Watch o'er Thy servants while they sleep.

And when the cord shall be unwound
With which our guilty race is bound,
Grant that we be not crushed beneath
The weight of everlasting death.

Ye Choirs of New Jerusalem.

(Chorus Novæ Jerusalem.)

By St. Fulbert of Chartres, who died about 1029. He was a man of very wide and varied attainments, and became distinguished throughout France for his abilities and wisdom. His advice was sought by kings and princes. He conducted a theological college at Chartres, and was consecrated bishop of that diocese. His writings which remain consist of hymns, letters, sermons, and theological treatises. The following version is taken from "Hymns Ancient and Modern," where it is altered from a translation by an unknown writer. There is another translation in Dr. Neale's "Mediæval Hymns."

YE choirs of New Jerusalem,
    Your sweetest notes employ,
The Paschal victory to hymn
    In strains of holy joy.

For Juda's Lion bursts His chains,
    Crushing the serpent's head;
And cries aloud, through death's domains,
    To wake the imprisoned dead.

Devouring depths of hell their prey
    At His command restore;
His ransomed hosts pursue their way
    Where Jesus goes before.

Triumphant in His glory now,
  To Him all power is given;
To Him in one Communion bow
  All saints in earth and heaven.

While we, His soldiers, praise our King,
  His mercy we implore,
Within His Palace bright to bring
  And keep us evermore.

All glory to the Father be;
  All glory to the Son;
All glory, Holy Ghost, to Thee,
  While endless ages run.
                    Alleluia! Amen.

Praise to Christ with Suppliant Voices.

(Laudes Christo redempti voce.)

A Prose of the eleventh century, translated by RICHARD FREDERICK LITTLEDALE.

PRAISE to Christ, with suppliant voices,
  Let His ransomed people sing:
Let the world which now rejoices
  Bless the Son of God, its King.

Ye, of Heaven's shrine the warders,
  Fellow-citizens of earth,
Standing in your ninefold orders,
  Join us to your festal mirth.

Sing aloud, O highest regions!
  Lowest deeps, your echoes raise!
To the Lord, in glad allegiance,
  Let all spirits give their praise.
God, as Man Himself concealing,
  Born in flesh to save mankind,
Bearing shame for sinners' healing,
  Yet as God in wonders shined.

With our human form invested,
  Truly Man, He dwelt below,
And no Godhead manifested
  At the tempting of the foe.
Craft with wisdom He defeated,
  And the knots of sin untied;
On the Cross, His work completed,
  There for us a Victim died.

To His Father sacrificing,
  By His death He sin hath slain:
Now, with noble pomp arising,
  From the depths He comes again;

Comes victorious over evil,
   Spoiling hell of all its prey,
Binding in His chains the Devil,
   On this glad triumphant day, —

Day which brightest radiance giveth,
   Now that Egypt's gloom is o'er
When He rose, Who ever liveth
   In the flesh which Mary bore:
Christ, Who here with mortals tarried,
   While the straying sheep He sought,
Which, upon his shoulders carried,
   To the Father He hath brought.

Jesu, the Very Thought of Thee.

(*Jesu, Dulcis Memoria.*)

By St. Bernard of Clairvaux, born in Fontaine, Burgundy, in 1091; died in 1153. He has been called the best and greatest man of his age, and Luther speaks of him as "the best monk that ever lived." He was the son of a nobleman, and was educated at the University of Paris. His tastes early inclined him to a monastic life; and, after three years spent in the Cistercian monastery of Citeaux, at the age of twenty-five he was appointed abbot of a new monastery at Clairvaux. This position he retained till his death, declining repeated offers of high preferment. He was often appealed to for counsel by kings and popes, and it was through his persuasion that the King of France undertook the crusade of 1146. The following is the first part of his Jubilation on the Name of Jesus, a hymn of about two hundred lines, which Dr. Schaff characterizes as the sweetest and most evangelical of the middle ages. The translation is by Edward Caswall. There are translations by Neale, Mrs. Charles, and others; but Mr. Caswall's is the sweetest and smoothest. In Dr. Schaff's "Christ in Song," in "Hymns Ancient and Modern," and in nearly all hymn-books, — for the lines have found their way into universal hymnology, — only the first four or five verses of this part are given. The last four verses entitle it to a place with Easter poems, and are quite too beautiful to be cast aside. The quotation is taken directly from Mr. Caswall's volume of "Hymns and Poems," with the lines which have been mutilated or marred by the hymn-menders restored.

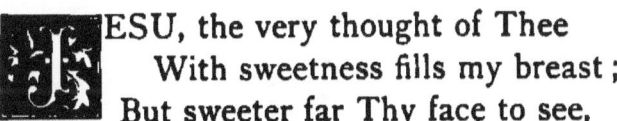
ESU, the very thought of Thee
    With sweetness fills my breast;
But sweeter far Thy face to see,
  And in Thy presence rest.

Nor voice can sing, nor heart can frame,
  Nor can the memory find,

46 JESU, THE VERY THOUGHT OF THEE.

A sweeter sound than Thy blest name,
   O Saviour of mankind!

O hope of every contrite heart!
   O joy of all the meek!
To those who fall, how kind Thou art!
   How good to those who seek!

But what to those who find? Ah, this
   Nor tongue nor pen can show:
The love of Jesus, what it is,
   None but His lovers know.

O Jesu, Light of all below!
   Thou Fount of life and fire!
Surpassing all the joys we know,
   And all we can desire!

Thee will I seek, at home, abroad,
   Who everywhere art nigh;
Thee in my bosom's cell, O Lord,
   As on my bed I lie.

With Mary to Thy tomb I'll haste,
   Before the dawning skies;
And all around, with longing, cast
   My soul's inquiring eyes;

Beside Thy grave will make my moan,
    And sob my heart away;
Then at Thy feet sink trembling down,
    And there adoring stay;

Nor from my tears and sighs refrain,
    Nor those dear feet release,
My Jesu, till from Thee I gain
    Some blessed word of peace!

𝕷o, t𝔥e 𝕮ates of 𝕯eat𝔥 are 𝕭roken.

(Mortis portis fractis, fortis.)

By PETER THE VENERABLE, born in Auvergne, in 1092 or 1094, of a noble family; died in 1156. He was elected abbot of Clugny in 1122, and it was with him that Abelard found shelter after the condemnation of his errors. He was a contemporary of Bernard of Clairvaux, and engaged in a keen controversy with him over the relative merits of the Clugniac and Cistercian monks. He gave to Christendom its first accurate translation of the Koran, and he wrote a refutation of Mahometanism. The following translation is by Mrs. CHARLES.

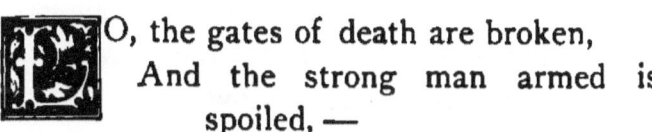O, the gates of death are broken,
    And the strong man armed is spoiled, —
Of his armor, which he trusted,
    By the Stronger Arm despoiled.
        Vanquished is the prince of hell,
        Smitten by the Cross he fell.

Then the purest light resplendent
    Shone those seats of darkness through,
When, to save whom he created,
    God willed to create anew.

That the sinner might not perish,
    For him the Creator dies;
By Whose death our dark lot changing,
    Life again for us doth rise.

Satan groaned, defeated then,
When the Victor ransomed men;
Fatal was to him the strife,
Unto man the source of life;
      Captured as he seized his prey,
      He is slain as he would slay.

Thus the King all hell hath vanquished
    Gloriously and mightily;
On the first day leaving Hades,
    Victor He returns on high.

Thus God brought man back to heaven,
    When He rose from out the grave,
The pure primal life bestowing,
    Which creating first He gave.

By the sufferings of his Maker,
    To his perfect Paradise
The first dweller thus returneth,
    Wherefore these glad songs arise.

Now the World's Fresh Dawn of Birth.

(Mundi Renovatio.)

By ADAM OF ST. VICTOR, whom Neale and Trench agree in regarding as the greatest of mediæval poets. He was born in Brittany,—in what year is uncertain,—and died about the year 1192. He was the author of more than a hundred sequences, which were collected and published by M. Gautier in 1858. His hymns are full of Old-Testament allusions, employed as types to illustrate New-Testament truths; and the theological often predominates over the devotional interest. But his verse has a rich melody, and an exquisite art and variety, and abounds in deep and tender feeling. The following fine translation is by P. S. WORSLEY.

NOW the world's fresh dawn of birth
    Teems with new rejoicings rife:
Christ is rising, and on earth
    All things with Him rise to life.
Feeling this memorial day,
Him the elements obey,
    Serve, and lay aside their strife.

Gleamy fire flits to and fro,
    Throbs the everlasting air,
Water without pause doth flow,
    And the earth stands firm and fair;
Light creations upward leap,
Heavier to the centre keep,
    All things renovation share.

Clearer are the skies above,
    And more quiet is the sea;
Each low wind is full of love,
    Our own vale is blooming free;
Dryness flushing into green,
Warm delight where frost hath been,
    For spring cometh tenderly.

Melted is the ice of death,
    And the world's prince driven away;
From amidst us vanisheth
    All his old tyrannic sway.
He, who sought to clasp more tight
That wherein he held no right,
    Fails of his peculiar prey.

Life is vanquisher of Death,
    And the joy man lost of old,
That he now recovereth,
    Even Paradise to hold.
For the cherub keeping ward,
By the promise of the Lord,
Turns the many-flaming sword,
    And the willing gates unfold.

Welcome the Triumphal Token.

(*Hæc est Dies Triumphalis.*)

By ADAM OF ST VICTOR. Translated by P. S. WORSLEY. (See note to the preceding hymn.)

WELCOME the triumphal token, —
    Day to ruined world how sweet,
When the foeman's power was broken,
    And our ills found comfort meet!
Know ye not this day so splendid,
    Shining with so fair a crown,
Witnessed Sin's dominion ended,
    And the Evil One cast down?

Then, the Prince of Darkness flying,
    Every baneful charm did cease;
Health came to the sick and dying,
    Rose on earth the reign of peace;
Death the sting of death undoing,
    Hope of life returned to-day;
Sin's stronghold was hurled to ruin,
    And pollution chased away.

Since, then, Christ our souls hath cherished
    In a union such as this,

And on earth hath freely perished
  For the things we wrought amiss,
Lightly may we hymn His story,
  And our Paschal banquet spread;
Heart, word, work, proclaim His glory,
  Rising with Him from the dead.

Hail the Much-Remembered Day!

(Ecce Dies celebris!)

By ADAM OF ST. VICTOR. Translated by Rev. J. M. NEALE, D.D.

HAIL the much-remembered Day!
  Night from morning flies away;
    Life the chains of Death hath burst:
Gladness, welcome! Grief, begone!
Greater glory draweth on
  Than confusion at the first.
Flies the shadowy from the true:
Flies the ancient from the new:
  Comfort hath each tear dispersed.

Hail, our Pascha, that wast dead!
What preceded in the Head,
  That each member hopes to gain;

Christ, our newer Pascha now,
Late in death content to bow,
   When the spotless Lamb was slain.

. . . .

From the Cross's pole of glory
Flows the must of ancient story
   In the Church's wine-vat stored:
From the press, now trodden duly,
Gentile first-fruits gathered newly
   Drink the precious liquor poured.

Sackcloth, worn with foul abuses,
Passes on to royal uses;
Grace in that garb at length we see,
The Flesh hath conquered misery.
They, by whom their monarch perished,
Lost the kingdom that they cherished;
And, for a sign and wonder, Cain
Is set, who never shall be slain.

Reprobated and rejected
Was this Stone, that, now elected,
For a Trophy stands erected,
   And a precious Corner-stone:
Sin's, not Nature's, termination,
He creates a new creation,
And, Himself their colligation,
   Binds two peoples into one.

Give we glory to the Head,
O'er the members love be shed!

Behold the Day the Lord hath made!

(Salve, Dies Dierum Gloria.)

By ADAM OF ST. VICTOR. Translated by H. R. B., in Rev. Orby Shipley's "Lyra Messianica."

BEHOLD the Day the Lord hath made!
That peerless day which cannot fade;
That day of light, that day of joy,
Of glory which shall never cloy.

The day on which the world was framed
Has signal honor ever claimed;
But Christ, arising from the dead,
Unrivalled brightness o'er it shed.

In hope of their celestial choice,
Now let the sons of light rejoice:
Christ's members in their lives declare
What likeness to their Head they bear.

For solemn is our feast to-day,
And solemn are the vows we pay:

THE DAY THE LORD HATH MADE.

This day's surpassing greatness claims
Surpassing joy, surpassing aims.

The Paschal victory displays
The glory of our festal days;
Which type and shadow dimly bore,
In promise to the saints of yore.

The veil is rent; and lo! unfold
The things the ancient Law foretold:
The figure from the substance flies,
And light the shadow's place supplies.

The type the spotless Lamb conveyed,
The goat, where Israel's sins were laid;
Messiah, purging our offence,
Disclosed in all their hidden sense.

By freely yielding up His breath,
He freed us from the bonds of death;
Who on that Prey forbidden flew,
And lost the prey that was his due.

The ills on sinful flesh that lay
His sinless flesh hath done away,
Which, blooming fresh on that third morn,
Assurance gave to souls forlorn.

O wondrous Death of Christ! may we
Be made to live to Christ by Thee!
O deathless Death, destroy our sin,
Give us the prize of life to win!

Christ, upon the Friday Slain.

(*Sexta passus feria.*)

By ADAM OF ST. VICTOR. Translated by RICHARD FREDERIC LITTLE-
DALE, D.C.L. See the biographical notice prefixed to the hymn, "Our
Paschal Joy at last is here."

CHRIST, upon the Friday slain,
When three days were past again,
  Rose victorious,
And, triumphant o'er the Tomb,
Lifts His loved ones out of gloom,
  Makes them glorious.

For the people of His Name,
He, upon the cross of shame,
  Dead was lying:
In the grave a while He lay,
Then, at dawning of the day,
  Rose undying.

In His passion and His cross,
With a bulwark sure from loss
    We are gifted :
By His resurrection bright,
From the grave of sin and night
    We are lifted.

Offered up for sinners, Christ
As their sacrifice sufficed
    Unrepeated :
By the precious blood He spilt,
Jesus washed our souls from guilt,
    Hell defeated.

Once He lay within the grave,
Lest the race He came to save
    Twice should perish :
Now He opens Heaven wide,
Comes to every mourner's side, —
    Comes to cherish.

He the Lion, strong in fight,
Rising up to-day, His might
    Forth is telling ;
With the arms of righteousness,
Satan, Prince of wickedness,
    Ever quelling.

Now is come the Lord's own day,
Whereon He hath washed away
  Earth's pollution;
Whereon death was slain in strife,
And the foe hath made of life
  Restitution.

So, from hearts made pure from stain,
Now the Alleluia strain
  Doubly pealeth:
Now all evil hath its close,
And the life which Heaven knows
  God revealeth.

In the world's late eventide,
Raise Thou up Thy servants tried,
  Jesu Holy:
May this glad and festal day
Thy salvation bring for aye
  To the lowly!

Purge we out the Ancient Leaven.

(*Zyma vetus expurgetur.*)

By ADAM OF ST. VICTOR. Translated by REV. J. M. NEALE, D.D. The original contains thirteen stanzas, of which we give only the first three and the last two, — the remainder of the sequence being taken up with a somewhat subtle application of Old-Testament types.

PURGE we out the ancient leaven,
That the feast of earth and heaven
    We may celebrate aright.
On to-day our hope stands founded:
Moses teacheth how unbounded
    Is its virtue and its might.

This day Egypt's treasure spoiled,
And the Hebrews freed, that toiled,
    Pressed with bondage and in chains,
From the mortar, brick, and stubble:
Heaviest toil and sorest trouble
    Had they known in Zoan's plains.

Now the voice of exultation,
Now the triumph of salvation,
    Free and wide its tidings flings.
This is the day the Lord hath made; the day
That bids our sin and sorrow flee away;
    Life and light and health that brings.

Death and life have striven newly:
Jesus Christ hath risen truly;
And with Christ ascended duly,
    Many a witness that He lives:
Dawn of newness, happy morrow,
Wipes away our eve of sorrow:
Since from death our life we borrow,
    Brightest joy the season gives.

Jesu, Victor, Life, and Head;
Jesu, Way Thy people tread;
By Thy death from death released,
Call us to the Paschal Feast,
    That with boldness we may come:
Living Water, Bread undying,
Vine, each branch with life supplying,
Thou must cleanse us, Thou must feed us,
From the second death must lead us
    Upward to our heavenly home!

Still thy Sorrow, Magdalena!

(Pone luctum, Magdalena!)

A sweet and jubilant hymn, of uncertain date and authorship. In "Lyra Messianica," and in Dr. Schaff's "Christ in Song," the name of the author is not given; and by Mrs. Charles it is ascribed to Adam of St. Victor ("Voice of Christian Life in Song," p. 182). The original may be found in Trench's "Sacred Latin Poetry," p. 159. There are several translations, by Mrs. Charles, W. J. C., and others; but the following — contributed by Rev. Dr. EDWARD A. WASHBURN to "Christ in Song" — is much the best. Dr. Washburn was born at Boston, April 16, 1819; graduated at Harvard University 1838; studied theology at Andover and New Haven: was rector of St. Paul's Episcopal Church, Newburyport, 1844-51; rector of St. John's, Hartford, 1853-62, and professor of church polity in Berkeley Divinity School, Middletown; rector of St. Mark's, Philadelphia, 1862-65; from 1865 to date, rector of Calvary Church, New York.

TILL thy sorrow, Magdalena!
  Wipe the teardrops from thine eyes:
  Not at Simon's board thou kneelest,
Pouring thy repentant sighs:
All with thy glad heart rejoices;
All things sing, with happy voices,
    Hallelujah!

Laugh with rapture, Magdalena!
  Be thy drooping forehead bright:
Banished now is every anguish,
  Breaks anew thy morning light:

Christ from death the world hath freed;
He is risen, is risen indeed:
        Hallelujah!

Joy! exult, O Magdalena!
   He hath burst the rocky prison:
Ended are the days of darkness:
   Conqueror hath He arisen.
Mourn no more the Christ departed;
Run to welcome Him, glad-hearted:
        Hallelujah!

Lift thine eyes, O Magdalena!
   See! thy living Master stands;
See His face, as ever, smiling;
   See those wounds upon His hands,
On His feet, His sacred side, —
Gems that deck the Glorified:
        Hallelujah!

Live, now live, O Magdalena!
   Shining is thy new-born day;
Let thy bosom pant with pleasure,
   Death's poor terror flee away;
Far from thee the tears of sadness:
Welcome love, and welcome gladness!
        Hallelujah!

Now Thy Gentle Lamb, O Sion!

(Mitis Agnus, Leo Fortis.)

A hymn of uncertain date, translated by HENRY TREND, D.D.

NOW thy gentle Lamb, O Sion,
    Shows the strength of Judah's Lion;
        Hell's stern fetters hold him not:
Dawns the third day o'er His prison,
And our mighty Saviour, risen,
        Makes us share His glorious lot.

Holy women, with devotion
Such as springs from love's emotion,
        Bring sweet unguents to His tomb:
There, O wonderful transition!
Worthy of the heavenly vision,
        Glory meets them in the gloom.

One in faith that scorns defection,
Equal in their warm affection
        For His Name Whose grave they seek,
Back they see the stone is taken,
And the opened tomb forsaken,
        Whence they hear an Angel speak:—

Fear not, loving souls; but going
Quickly back, the vision showing,
   Say to Peter and the rest,
Jesus lives, o'er death victorious,
Now to reign forever glorious,
   In the regions of the blest!

Joy! O Joy! Ye Broken-hearted!

(Cedant justi signa luctus.)

An ancient hymn, of uncertain date and authorship; translated by HERBERT KYNASTON, D.D. Dr. Kynaston was born at Warwick, Nov. 23, 1809; was educated at Westminster and Oxford; became tutor, philological lecturer, and master of the schools; was ordained in 1834; became curate of Culham; held successively the livings of St. Botolph, Aldgate, and of St. Nicholas Cole Abbey, London; and, in 1853, was appointed a prebend of St. Paul's. He is the author of a hundred or more original hymns and translations.

JOY! O joy! ye broken-hearted!
   Joy! the dreadful sea is parted:
      Here and there the ramping wave
      Frowns beside an empty grave.
With His blood the Lamb hath laved us,
With His passing Christ has saved us,
      Shouting, on the Red-sea shore,
      Alleluia! evermore.

Loud above the billows' thunder
Sound the chains He rives asunder:
    Saints below, of ancient days,
    Glisten with His rising rays:
Saints who died before they saw Him,
Yearn to rise on earth before Him;
    Yearn to take the form He wore:
    Alleluia! evermore.

All our marbled slumber breaking,
From our sinful dreams awaking,
    From our worldly cerements free,
    Jesus, make us rise with Thee!
Thee, our death, hell's portals rending,
Thee, our life, to God ascending,
    All our blessings to restore,
    Alleluia! evermore.

𝔄lleluia! 𝔄lleluia!

(Alleluia! Alleluia! Finita jam sunt prœlia.)

A spirited hymn, the author of which is unknown. By H. A. Daniel, in his "Thesaurus Hymnologicus," it is referred to the twelfth century; by Dr. J. M. NEALE, who translates it, to the thirteenth. A less-spirited version, by Rev. Francis Pott, may be found in "Hymns Ancient and Modern."

LLELUIA! Alleluia!
Finished is the battle now,
The crown is on the Victor's brow.
  Hence with sadness!
  Sing with gladness,
      Alleluia!

Alleluia! Alleluia!
After sharp death that Him befell,
Jesus Christ hath harrowed hell!
  Earth is singing,
  Heaven is ringing,
      Alleluia!

Alleluia! Alleluia!
On the third morning He arose,
Bright with victory o'er His foes.
  Sing we lauding,
  And applauding,
      Alleluia!

Alleluia! Alleluia!
He hath closed hell's brazen door,
And heaven is open evermore!
    Hence with sadness!
    Sing with gladness,
        Alleluia!

Alleluia! Alleluia!
Lord, by Thy wounds we call on Thee,
So from ill death to set us free;
    That our living
    Be thanksgiving.
        Alleluia!

Christ the Lord is Risen To-day.

(*Victimæ Paschali laudes.*)

An anonymous hymn, based upon a Latin Sequence of the twelfth or thirteenth century. From Archbishop Manning's Collection for the use of St. Mary of the Angels Church, Bayswater.

CHRIST the Lord is risen to-day;
Christians, haste your vows to pay;
Offer ye your praises meet
At the Paschal Victim's feet.
For the sheep the Lamb hath bled,
Sinless in the sinner's stead:

"Christ is risen," to-day we cry;
Now He lives, no more to die.

Christ, the Victim undefiled,
Man to God hath reconciled;
Whilst in strange and awful strife
Met together Death and Life;
Christians, on this happy day,
Haste with joy your vows to pay;
"Christ is risen," to-day we cry,
Now He lives, no more to die.

Christ, Who once for sinners bled,
Now the First-born from the dead,
Throned in endless might and power,
Lives and reigns for evermore.
Hail, eternal Hope on high!
Hail, Thou King of victory!
Hail, Thou Prince of Life adored!
Help and save us, gracious Lord!

Forth to the Paschal Victim, Christians, bring.

(Victimæ Paschali laudes.)

A more literal translation of the same Sequence, by EDWARD CASWALL.

FORTH to the Paschal Victim, Christians, bring
  Your sacrifice of praise.

The Lamb redeems the sheep;
  And Christ, the Sinless One,
  Hath to the Father sinners reconciled.

Together Death and Life
  In a strange conflict strove;
  The Prince of Life, who died,
  Now lives and reigns.

What thou sawest, Mary, say,
As thou wentest on the way.

I saw the tomb wherein the Living One had lain;
I saw His glory as He rose again;
Napkin and linen clothes, and Angels twain;

Yea, Christ is risen, my hope, and He
Will go before you into Galilee.

We know that Christ indeed has risen from
    the grave:
Hail, thou King of victory!
Have mercy, Lord, and save.

Spring is in its Beauty glowing.

(Ecce tempus est vernale.)

Translated from a Sequence of the thirteenth century by HENRY TREND, D.D. See the biographical notice prefixed to the hymn, "Hail, Day of Joyous Rest!"

SPRING is in its beauty glowing,
  When the tree unique in growing,
  Through the world its branches
    throwing,
Bears our wondrous Ransom, showing
  Man o'er death victorious.

Urged by Jews of cruel feeling,
Men His mystic fruit are peeling;
O'er the cross His blood is stealing;
Heaven grows dark, the earth is reeling,
  At this deed notorious.

Charged with blasphemy and treason,
See Him scourged, and suffering lesion
From the crown of thorns' adhesion,
Tasting gall, and without reason
    Bearing scoffs opprobrious.

But while frantic Jews are crying,
Lead Him off for crucifying!
While in torments He is dying,
To our race in misery lying
    Comes salvation glorious.

Saints of God, from your dejection
Rise in faith and strong affection;
Give your hearts to joy's direction;
Lo! the day of resurrection
    Dawns in brightness o'er us!

Ye Sons and Daughters of the King.

(O Filii et Filiæ!)

An anonymous hymn from the Latin of the thirteenth century, translated by Dr. NEALE. The compilers of "Hymns Ancient and Modern" have altered and condensed Dr. Neale's version, giving it somewhat more of smoothness at the cost of strength and simplicity. Caswall has a translation, beginning, "Ye Sons and Daughters of the Lord."

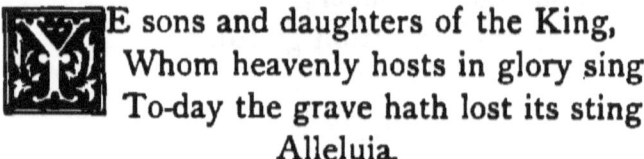E sons and daughters of the King,
Whom heavenly hosts in glory sing,
To-day the grave hath lost its sting!
   Alleluia.

On that first morning of the week,
Before the day began to break,
They went their buried Lord to seek.
   Alleluia.

Both Mary, as it came to pass,
And Mary Magdalene it was,
And Mary, wife of Cleopas.
   Alleluia.

An Angel clad in white was he
That sate and spake unto the three,
"Your Lord is gone to Galilee!"
   Alleluia.

When John the Apostle heard the fame,
He to the tomb with Peter came;
But in the way outran the same.
              Alleluia.

That night the Apostles met in fear:
Amidst them came their Lord most dear,
And said, "Peace be unto all here!"
              Alleluia.

When Didymus had after heard
That Jesus had fulfilled His word,
He doubted if it were the Lord.
              Alleluia.

"Thomas, behold My side," saith He;
"My hands, my feet, my body, see:
And doubt not, but believe in Me."
              Alleluia.

No longer Didymus denied:
He saw the hands, the feet, the side:
"Thou art my Lord and God!" he cried.
              Alleluia.

Blessed are they that have not seen,
And yet whose faith hath constant been:
In life eternal they shall reign.
              Alleluia.

On this most holy Day of days
Be laud and jubilee and praise :
To God both hearts and voices raise.
    Alleluia.

And we with Holy Church unite,
As is both meet and just and right,
In Glory to the King of Light.
    Alleluia.

Saints on Earth, and Saints in Light.

(Cæli choris perennibus.)

A hymn for Lauds, translated by Rev. PHIPPS ONSLOW, and contributed to "Lyra Messianica." Mr. Onslow was born about 1824, and graduated at Oxford in 1846. He was ordained in 1847, served as curate of Longdon from 1847 to 1859, and has been rector of Upper Sapey, Herefordshire, since the latter date.

SAINTS on earth, and saints in light,
In your songs of praise unite ;
Praise to Christ, the Heavenly King,
O'er death's bondage triumphing.

Flesh and soul death's law divides,
Still the Word with each abides ;
Flesh and soul death rends in twain,
He reknits their life again.

Whom the Virgin's womb revealed, —
Womb of Virgin ne'er unsealed, —
From the sealèd cave outbroke,
In death's womb to life awoke.

Love, the sweetest known on high,
Sternly, Jesu, bade Thee die;
Love, the Priest, Thy bitter death
To the Father offereth.

Jesu, risen Saviour, give
Grace Thy risen life to live, —
Grace, from sin's dark fetters free,
Works of love to offer Thee.

Words may not Thy Glory tell.

(*Te quanta Victor funeris.*)

A vesper hymn, translated by W. H. D., in "Lyra Messianica."

WORDS may not Thy glory tell,
Conqueror of death and hell,
Whom the Cross but lately bore,
Now alive for evermore.
Marred by cruel blows wast Thou:
Stars have no such glory now.

Though untouched by any need,
Still with men Thou deign'st to feed.
Needs no more the uttered word:
Wind and wave no less have heard,
Own their Lord, and pathway meet
Spread before His passing feet.
Fleshly fetters now forgot,
Doors of brass may stay Thee not;
Other, yet the same — but free
To come and go as liketh Thee.
Lord! our hope Thou biddest rise,
Grasping life beyond the skies,
Where Thy glory we shall view,
In Thine image clothed anew.

Jesus hath Vanished: all in Vain.

(*Erumpe tandem juste dolor.*)

This quaint and beautiful piece appears among the translations of EDWARD CASWALL, without any intimation as to the authorship or date of the original. Mr. Caswall, to whom we owe some of the finest translations that we have from the Latin sacred poets, was born in 1814, at Yately, in Hampshire, England. He graduated at Oxford in 1836, and was ordained priest in 1839. In 1847 he joined the Church of Rome, and three years later was admitted into the Congregation of the Oratory at Birmingham, where he has since remained. He has published a volume of "Hymns and Poems," and several prose works.

MARY MAGDALEN.

JESUS hath vanished : all in vain
I search for Him, and search again,
Seeking to relieve my pain.
My sobs the garden fill,
My sighs in tears distil ;
My heart is breaking. Where is He?
Who hath hid my love from me?

JESUS.

Who is this in wild disorder,
Running over bed and border?
O lady, speak!
Declare, declare,
What floweret fair

Hither you come to seek;
Wherefore these piteous tears bedew your
    cheek!

MARY MAGDALEN.

Say, O gentle gardener, say,
Where have they borne my Lord away?
    In what deep grove or glade
    Have they His body laid?
    Where is that lily sweet,
    The Son of God most dear?
    Tell me, oh, tell me where!
That I may go, and kiss His sacred feet,
And my true Spouse adore,
And to His Mother's arms the Son restore!

JESUS.

Mary, what blindness hath come o'er thee!
I, thy Jesus, stand before thee, —
    I, that immortal flower
    Of Nazareth's fair bower;
I, amid thousands, the Elect alone;
I, thy beloved; I, thine own!

MARY MAGDALEN.

Jesu, Master! Thy dear sight
Quite dissolves me with delight!
O Joy of joys! to see thy face,
And those celestial feet embrace!

JESUS.

Touch me not yet: the hour is drawing nigh
When thou shalt see Me glorified on high;
Then in Mine endless presence shalt thou rest,
And, drinking of My light, live on forever blest!

Hail the Holy Day of Days!

(*Hæc est sancta solemnitas solemnitatum.*)

A sequence from a manuscript missal translated by JOHN WILLIAM HEWETT, in "Lyra Messianica." Mr. Hewett was born about 1828, graduated at Trinity College, Cambridge, in 1849, was ordained deacon in the same year, and priest the year following. He held the position of tutor of St. Nicholas College, Shoreham, for several years, and was afterward curate of Bloxham and of Whitwick. He is the author of several antiquarian, historical, and ecclesiastical works, of some original hymns, and of one or two volumes of translations of Latin hymns.

HAIL the holy day of days!
High the song of triumph raise;
To the Saviour's glory tell,
How the cross hath vanquished hell,
And the empire, old and strong,
Satan's power had held so long.
By the precious blood are we
Now redeemed of Christ, and free:

High thanksgiving therefore raise,
Sing the great Redeemer's praise.
King of kings, Thy saints unite
To the choir of Angels bright;
Hear them when they make their prayer,
For Thy worship is their care.
Show them, Lord, Thy tender grace,
All the sweetness of Thy face.
Thou, Who wouldst not man should lie,
Under righteous doom to die,
Who, for man, didst stoop so low,
Death Thyself to undergo, —
Thou hast changed that law of doom,
Rising from Thy sacred tomb.
Now, Thy bitter passion done,
Thou, the well-beloved Son
Of the Father, throned on high,
Rulest all below the sky.
Alleluia! Lord, we sing,
Jesu, Christ, Redeemer, King!

Smile Praises, O Sky!

(Plaudite cœli.)

The author and the date of the following are unknown; it is not earlier than the fourteenth, and is possibly as recent as the sixteenth century. The translation is by Mrs. ELIZABETH CHARLES, and is contained in her "Voice of Christian Life in Song." Mrs. Charles is the daughter of John Rundle, Esq., of Tavistock, Devonshire, England, where she was born. She has written a very popular series of narratives, the scenes and characters in which are largely drawn from modern religious history. She has enriched hymnology by original hymns and translations; and the work from which the following is taken is one of considerable value and interest.

SMILE praises, O sky!
   Soft breathe them, O air!
Below and on high,
   And everywhere.
The black troop of storms
   Has yielded to calm;
Tufted blossoms are peeping,
   And early palm.

Arouse thee, O spring!
   Ye flowers, come forth,
With thousand hues tinting
   The soft green earth;

Ye violets tender,
   And sweet roses bright,
Gay Lent-lilies blended
   With pure lilies white.

Sweep, tides of rich music,
   The full veins along;
And pour in full measure,
   Sweet lyres, your song.
Sing, sing, for He liveth, —
   He lives, as He said;
The Lord has arisen
   Unharmed from the dead.

Clap, clap your hands, mountains!
   Ye valleys, resound!
Leap, leap for joy, fountains!
   Ye hills, catch the sound.
All triumph! He liveth, —
   He lives, as He said;
The Lord hath arisen
   Unharmed from the dead.

Now Morning Lifts her Dewy Veil.

(*Ad templa nos rursus vocat.*)

A translation of a Latin hymn of uncertain date and authorship. This version is by Rev. JOHN CHANDLER (born about 1805, and, as late as 1872, still living in Surrey, England). It is a variation — considerably improved and strengthened — upon a translation of the same hymn by Rev. Isaac Williams (born in 1802, died in 1865). There is still another translation by Edward Caswall, beginning, "Again the Sunday morn."

NOW Morning lifts her dewy veil,
   With new-born blessings crowned:
   Oh, haste we, then, her light to hail
In courts of holy ground!

But Christ, triumphant o'er the grave,
   Shines more divinely bright:
Oh, sing we then His power to save,
   And walk we in His light!

When from the swaddling bands of shade
   Sprang forth the world so fair,
In robes of brilliancy arrayed,
   Oh, what a Power was there!

When He, who gave His guiltless Son
   A guilty world to spare,

84 *NOW MORNING LIFTS HER DEWY VEIL.*

Restored to life the Holy One,
  Oh, what a Love was there!

When forth from its Creator's hand
  The earth in beauty stood,
All decked with light at His command,
  He saw, and called it good.

But still more lovely in His sight,
  The earth still fairer stood,
When the Holy Lamb had washed it white
  In His atoning blood.

Still, as the morning rays return,
  To the pious soul 'tis given
In fancy's mirror to discern
  The radiant domes of heaven.

But, now that our eternal Sun
  Hath shed His beams abroad,
In Him we see the Holy One,
  And mount at once to God.

Oh, holy, blessed Three in One!
  May Thy pure light be given,
That we the paths of death may shun,
  And keep the road to Heaven!

O Thou, the Heavens' Eternal King!

(Rex sempiterne cælitum.)

From the Roman Breviary. Translated by EDWARD CASWALL. There are other versions, of which that by the compilers of "Hymns Ancient and Modern," beginning, "O Christ, the Heavens' Eternal King," is the most familiar. Mr. Caswall's translation, however, excels it, both in strength and beauty

O THOU, the heavens' eternal King,
    Lord of the starry spheres!
Who with the Father equal art,
    From everlasting years:

All praise to Thy most holy Name,
    Who, when the world began,
Yoking the soul with clay, didst form,
    In Thine own image, man.

And praise to Thee, who, when the foe
    Had marred Thy work sublime,
Clothing Thyself in flesh, didst mould
    Our race a second time;

When from the tomb new-born, as from
    A virgin born before,

86 O THOU, THE HEAVENS' ETERNAL KING!

Thou, raising us from death with Thee,
    Didst us in Thee restore.

Eternal Shepherd! who Thy flock
    In Thy pure font dost lave,
Where souls are cleansed, and all their guilt
    Buried, as in a grave;

Jesu, who to the cross wast nailed,
    Our hopeless debt to pay, —
Jesu, who lavishly didst pour
    Thy blood for us away, —

Oh, from the wretched death of sin
    Keep us! so shalt Thou be
The everlasting Paschal joy
    Of all new-born in Thee.

To God the Father, with the Son
    Who from the grave arose,
And Thee, O Paraclete, be praise
    While age on ages flows!

Helped by the Almighty's Arm, at Last.

(*Forti tegente brachia.*)

From the Paris Breviary. Translated by JOHN DAVID CHAMBERS, in "Lauda Syon: Ancient Latin Hymns of the English and other Churches." Mr. Chambers was a graduate of Oxford in 1826, and has made a number of contributions to devotional literature.

HELPED by the Almighty's arm, at last
Behold the Red Sea's channel past,
Where He, with matchless prowess, broke
The infernal tyrant's hateful yoke.

Oh! therefore joyful thanks this day
Let us to Christ, our Champion, pay;
And round the Lamb's own board unite,
Arrayed in shining robes of white.

There duly may His sacred flesh
And hallowed blood our souls refresh;
Enkindling there the fire of love,
That we may live with Him above.

Henceforth our Passover is Christ;
Our Lamb, our Victim sacrificed:

As sprinkled with His blood we stand,
The angel stays his vengeful hand.

O worthiest Victim! born to reign;
By whom Death's very self is slain;
And, crushed before whose potent sway,
The gates of hell disgorge their prey!

Christ, from the grave's departing gloom,
To light hath issued from the tomb;
Down to the abyss the foe hath driven,
And oped the sanctuaries of heaven.

The Orient Beams of Easter Morn.

(Aurora lucis dum novæ.)

From the Paris Breviary. Translated by JOHN DAVID CHAMBERS, in "Lauda Syon."

THE orient beams of Easter morn
The glowing firmament adorn:
Let earth with joyous plaudits ring,
The Lamb's victorious triumphs sing.

He with His Blood — pellucid tide! —
This world from sin hath purified;

The Veil He rends, the Holiest lies
Revealed unto our ravished eyes!

To earth consigned, the noble Grain
Inert no longer may remain;
Scarce dead, behold It blooming fair,
A rich and wondrous harvest bear!

No more shall death the flesh destroy,
Sown in sure hope of future joy:
Our God to life the way hath led,
Who rose, the first-fruits of the dead.

So on the Cross with Jesus slain,
With Him revived to life again,
Shall this frail body rise, to rest
In His all-glorious image dressed.

Thou, Who to Save.

(Jesu, Redemptor sæculi.)

A hymn of the Paris Breviary, translated by Rev. ISAAC WILLIAMS. Mr. Williams was born in 1802; graduated at Oxford 1826; was ordained in 1831; held livings at Windrush, Oxford, and Bisley; suffered for many years from broken health; and died May 1, 1865. He was the author of a large number of hymns, original and translated, and of several devotional and homiletical works in prose.

HOU, Who to save
    The world didst die, and then Thy
        breath
Resume, to vanquish gloomy death,
    And kill the grave;

    O'er all below
Night reigns; our eyes are weighed with
    sleep:
Oh, from the wiles and watchings keep
    Of the great foe

    May rest, which lays
Care's lid, and labor's brow doth slake,
Quicken our hearts, more fresh to wake
    Unto Thy praise!

> Oh, be it given
> With Thee to die, on earth to love
> The better things which are above,
> And dwell in Heaven!

Christ with Mighty Triumph rises!

(Surgit Christus cum Trophæo.)

An Easter Sequence from the Missal of Tournay: sixteenth century. Translated by JOHN WILLIAM HEWETT. From "Lyra Mystica." See biographical note prefixed to the hymn, "Hail, the Holy Day of Days!"

CHRIST with mighty Triumph rises!
All the gates of Death surprises!
  From a Lamb a Lion strong.
Hell through all its depths is quaking;
Earth through all its graves is shaking:
  Raise on high the Victor's song!

Hail the Lamb! adore him greatly,
Who upon the Cross but lately
  For His helpless Sheep was slain:
By His Death He brought Salvation,
To the lost of every nation
  Showed the Way of Life again.

He alone His Passion bearing,
None His mighty Grief was sharing
   Save repentant Magdalene.
Tell us, Mary, 'mid thy weeping,
By the Cross thy station keeping,
   All the woes that thou hast seen. —

I beheld the Lord's Anointed
Bear the Stripes to sin appointed,
   Lifted on His Cross to die;
Saw the Lord His Thorn-crown wearing,
Grossest insult meekly bearing,
   Pale His cheek, and sunk His eye.

Through His Hands the nails were driven,
By the spear His Side was riven:
   Then He bowed His sacred Head,
And His Soul to God commended,
All His bitter Passion ended:
   Lo! the Lord of Life was dead. —

Tell us, Mary, all thy doing,
Still thy task of love pursuing,
   When the Saviour's Soul was fled. —
By the martyred Mother keeping,
While I soothed, I shared her weeping,
   Till unto her home I led:

Then, upon the hard earth falling,
Mourned I o'er that Scene appalling,
　　Mourned my Saviour's bitter Doom;
Then the fragrant spices blending,
Love's last precious care attending,
　　Hied me to the sacred Tomb:

Search for my Beloved making,
Him for Whom my heart was breaking,
　　All my searching proved in vain:
Then my Soul was newly troubled,
All my grief and care was doubled,
　　And my tears burst forth again. —

Weep not, Mary, now unduly;
Christ the Lord hath risen truly,
　　Broke the seal, and 'scaped the ward. —
Words of comfort ye have spoken;
And indeed no single token
　　Saw I of the risen Lord:

Shining Angels told the story, —
Here is not the Lord of Glory;
　　He is risen, as He said:
See unwound each linen cerement,
And yon token of endearment
　　Which enwrapped His sacred Head.

Yea, indeed, the Lord is risen!
Bursting from his narrow Prison;
  Hope in Him, ye Sons of men!
Risen Saviour, leave us never,
Show us **Love** and Pity ever;
  Alleluia! Lord! Amen.

Angels, to Our Jubilee.

(*Adeste, Cœlitum chori.*)

A hymn of NICHOLAS LE TOURNEAUX, a priest of Rouen, in 1686; translated by WILLIAM JOHN BLEW. Mr. Blew was born about 1810, and graduated at Oxford in 1832. He has held a living at St. John's, near Gravesend, Kent. He is the author of a translation of the Agamemnon of Æschylus, of a number of hymns and translations from the Latin, and of a compact but very valuable treatise on "Hymns and Hymn-Books."

ANGELS, to our Jubilee
  Haste, your sweetest songs awaking:
Christ amid the dead is free,
  Christ the rocky tomb is breaking.
Vain the guard around the grave;
  Vain the rulers' wild endeavor;
Vain the seal upon the cave
  Of the nation faithless ever.

Fear, away! no subtle spy
    Steals that form so sorely stricken:
He who willed the death to die
    Will with life Himself requicken.
Offspring of a Virgin's womb,
    Virgin-born He came, in token
That through Jewry's guarded tomb
    He should rise with seals unbroken.
Hanging on the inglorious tree,
    Mad with mocking lips they grieve Him, —
"Let him quit the Cross, and we
    Will the Son of God believe Him."
From the Cross He came not down,
    Yet He worked a mightier wonder:
Son of God the Saviour own;
    Dead, He smites grim death asunder.
Grant us, Lord, with Thee to die,
    And to rise at Thine uprising;
And to set our heart on high,
    Earth and all its joys despising.

Jesus Christ is Risen To-day.

(Surrexit Christus hodie.)

An anonymous hymn, written about 1750. Contained in "Hymns Ancient and Modern." Probably reproduced from a Latin hymn of the fifteenth century.

JESUS Christ is risen to-day, Alleluia!
Our triumphant holy day, Alleluia!
Who did once, upon the cross, Alleluia!
Suffer to redeem our loss, Alleluia!

Hymns of praise then let us sing, Alleluia!
Unto Christ, our heavenly King, Alleluia!
Who endured the Cross and Grave, Alleluia!
Sinners to redeem and save, Alleluia!

But the pain which He endured, Alleluia!
Our Salvation hath procured, Alleluia!
Now above the sky He's King, Alleluia!
Where the angels ever sing, Alleluia!
        Amen.

From the Russian.

The Golden Palace of my God.

By SEMEN SERGEJEWITSCH BOBROFF, the date of whose birth is unknown. He was an assessor of colleges, was educated at the University of Moscow, and began his career as a poet in 1784. In 1803 he published " The Chersonese, or a Summer's Day on the Tauric Peninsula;" in 1804, " Daybreak of the North," lyrical poems in four parts; in 1807, " The Ancient Night of the Universe, or the Blind Wanderer," a poem in four volumes. He died in 1810. He had a fiery imagination, and a fund of feeling, but was not always felicitous in expression, and his sublimity sometimes verges upon bombast. He was more familiar with English literature than any other Russian writer. The following hymn is sung in the Russian churches at midnight a week before Easter. The translation is by SIR JOHN BOWRING.

THE golden Palace of my God
    Towering above the clouds I see,
    Beyond the Cherubs' bright abode,
Higher than angels' thoughts can be.
How can I in those Courts appear
    Without a wedding-garment on?
Conduct me, thou Life-Giver, there, —
    Conduct me to Thy glorious throne!
And clothe me with Thy robes of light,
And lead me through Sin's darksome night,
    My Saviour and my God!

Why, Thou Never-Setting Light.

Also by BORROFF, translated by BOWRING. See note to the preceding. This also is a midnight hymn, and is sung in the Russian churches at Easter.

WHY, thou Never-Setting Light,
   Is thy brightness veiled from me?
Why does this unusual night
   Cloud thy blest benignity?
I am lost without thy ray:
   Guide my wandering footsteps, Lord!
Light my dark and erring way
   To the noontide of thy word!

From the Danish.

Arise, my Soul! awake from Sleep!

By THOMAS KINGO, who was born in Slangcrup in 1634; was appointed curate of Kirke-Helsinge in 1662, and priest at Slangcrup in 1668; was made Bishop of Funen in 1677; and died in 1703. He was the author of over two hundred quaint psalms and hymns, and was much beloved by his countrymen. He has been called the Dr. Watts of Denmark. The translator of this hymn and the two following is Mr. GILBERT TAIT. They are to be found in his collection of "The Hymns of Denmark."

ARISE, my soul! awake from sleep!
    Behold thy Saviour's grave!
    His loved ones, mourning, laid Him deep
In Death's devouring cave;
But from the tomb He valiant came,
And ever blessed be His name!

A cheering sound, an angel's voice,
    Proclaimeth from on high,
Our brother, Jesus, — oh, rejoice! —
    Could not Death's captive lie;
But from the tomb He valiant came,
And ever blessed be His name!

O sacred day, sublimest day!
    O mystery unheard!
Death's hosts, that claimed Him as their prey,
    He scattered with a word;

And from the tomb He valiant came,
And ever blessed be His name!

O holy, holy Paschal morn!
　　We triumphed have through thee:
Thou sweetenest Christ's torture, borne
　　Upon the fatal tree;
For from the tomb He valiant came,
And ever blessed be His name!

I boldly now defy thee, Death!
　　For thou hast lost thy sting;
Defy, O Hell! thy blasting breath,
　　All terrors thou canst bring;
For from the tomb He valiant came,
And ever blessed be His name!

The grave is dark, the grave is cold,
　　And I must slumber there;
But, risen, I shall Christ behold,
　　Christ's glories I shall share;
For from the tomb He valiant came,
And ever blessed be His name!

That I a welcome warm may win
　　From Jesus in the skies,
From the foul sepulchre of sin
　　May I as valiant rise
As from the tomb the Saviour came:
And ever blessed be His name!

From Death, Christ, on the Sabbath Morn.

By NICOLAI FREDERIK SEVERIN GRUNDTVIG, born at Udby, South Zealand, Sept 8, 1783. He studied classics and theology at Aarhuus, and became deeply interested in Icelandic literature. For several years he taught in Langeland, and wrote essays on the Edda, &c. In 1808 he published a polemic poem lashing the frivolity of the people of Copenhagen, also a work on Northern mythology. About this time his mind, always devout, became deeply and passionately religious, and he devoted himself unreservedly to the work of moral and religious reform. His "Probation Sermon" threw the clergy of Copenhagen into an uproar, and called down upon him their formal censure. In 1813, after a period of rest necessitated by illness and nervous excitement, he returned to Copenhagen, and preached conversion and faith to his countrymen; and in 1814, when the Allied Army overran Holstein, he renewed his patriotic and religious appeals. His earnestness provoked frequent attacks from the rationalistic clergy, who prevented his preferment. In 1822-26 he was resident chaplain of Our Saviour's Church at Christianshavn; and in 1839 was appointed clergyman of the Church of the Holy Ghost, Copenhagen. He was an indefaugable literary worker, and undertook laborious translations from Icelandic and Anglo-Saxon literature. His collection of psalms and hymns was published in 1841. Howitt likens him to John the Baptist crying in the wilderness, and characterizes him as "one of the giants of the North, burning with religious zeal." Miss Bremer placed him foremost among Danish bards and seers, and said of his hymns, that they gave new life to the church music of Denmark. The following is from Mr. Tait's "Hymns of Denmark."

FROM death, Christ, on the Sabbath morn,
    A conqueror arose;
And, when each Sabbath dawn is born,
    For death a healing grows.
This day proclaims an ended strife,
And Christ's benign and holy life,

By countless lips the wondrous tale
    Is told throughout the earth:
Ye that have ears to hear, oh, hail
    That tale with sacred mirth!
Awake, my soul! rise from the dead!
See life's grand light around thee shed!

Death trembles each sweet Sabbath hour:
    Death's brother, Darkness, quakes:
Christ's word speaks with divinest power;
    Christ's truth its silence breaks:
They vanquish with their valiant breath
The reign of Darkness and of Death.

O Christians, let us Joyful be!

By —— RAMUS, who is represented by several hymns in Mr. Tait's " Hymns of Denmark." The editor has made careful search in English and French histories of Danish Literature, and in various biographical dictionaries, but finds no mention of this author, whose place is doubtless among the minor sacred poets of Denmark.

O CHRISTIANS, let us joyful be!
    How sweet, how holy is this day!
Behold Him free, and boldly free, —
    Our Saviour, Christ, death's grandest prey!
He burst the fetters of the tomb,
And rose in triumph from the gloom.

For sin a bitter lot He chose;
  The Cross's pangs He willing bore;
First-fruits of them that slept, He rose;
  And we shall rise, to sleep no more.
Oh, comfort for each contrite soul,
To see away death's terrors roll!

To Thee, O loving God! we pray:
  May in our heart Thy Spirit dwell:
Oh, lead us in salvation's way;
  Teach us to feel that all is well;
And, when our earthly course is run,
Give us the kingdom Jesus won!

From the German.

There went Three Damsels ere Break of Day.

This quaint ballad was a favorite with devout Germans of the fourteenth century. The name of the author is not known. The translation is by CATHERINE WINKWORTH, who was born about 1825; and died July, 1878. English readers are indebted to her for many admirable translations of German hymns contained in her two series of "Lyra Germanica," and her history of "The Christian Singers of Germany."

THERE went three damsels ere break of day:
To the Holy Grave they took their way;
They fain would anoint the Lord once more,
As Mary Magdalene did before.   Alleluia!

The damsels each to other made moan,—
"Who will roll us away the stone,
That we may enter in amain
To anoint the Lord as we are fain?"

Full precious spices and salve they brought;
But, when they came to the spot they sought,
Behold, the grave doth open stand!
An angel sitteth on either hand!

"Ye maidens, be not filled with fear:
He whom ye seek, He is not here:
Behold, the raiment white and fair,
Which the Lord was wrapped in, lieth there.

"Ye maidens, do not here delay:
Ye must to Galilee away;
To Galilee ye now must go,
For there the Lord Himself will show."

But Mary Magdalene could not depart:
Seeking the Lord, she wept apart.
What saw she in a little while?
She saw our Lord upon her smile.

In garb and wise He met her there
As were He a gardener, and did bear
A spade within His holy hand,
As would He dig the garden land.

"Oh! tell me, gentle Gardener thou,
Where hast thou laid my Master now?
Where thou hast hidden Him, bid me know,
Or my heart must break beneath its woe."

Scarce could He speak a single word,
Ere she beheld it was the Lord:
She kneeleth down on the cold bare stone;
She hath found her Lord, and she alone.

"Touch me not, Mary Magdalene,
But tell the brethren what thou hast seen:
Touch me not now with human hand,
Until I ascend to my Father's land."
Alleluia!

Rejoice, Dear Christendom, To-day.

This hymn belongs in the same period as the preceding, but is an expansion of an earlier Easter sequence. Miss WINKWORTH is the translator.

REJOICE, dear Christendom, to-day;
    For Christ hath overcome:
  His bitter pains have passed away,
    And empty stands His tomb;
  Those bitter pains had been our lot,
  If Christ for us had borne them not.
Great bliss hath risen on us to-day:
Alleluia!

O Easter Day, our voices ne'er
    Can praise thee fittingly;
Since God, whose power all things declare,
    Such glory puts on thee:
    But let us keep thee as we can.
    Angels to-day rejoice with man,
When rose that Sun so wondrous fair:
Alleluia!

O Jesus Christ, our blessed Lord,
  We share Thy joy to-day!
All those who hear and keep Thy Word
  Are glad with Thee to-day!
  All Christian people now rejoice
  With freshened hearts and gladsome voice.
Glory to Thee, our Blessed Lord:
                              Alleluia!

Praise to the Father and the Son,
  And to the Holy Ghost:
For all the sins that we have done,
  To-day forgive us most;
  And give us peace and unity,
  From now to all eternity,
So sing we as the ages run:
                              Alleluia!

So Holy is this Day of Days.

This sequence is found about the same date as the preceding; and, in the old manuscripts which contain it, it is called "The Common Man's Processional." The translation is by Miss WINKWORTH.

S O holy is this day of days,
  No man can fill its meed of praise.
    Since the Holy Son of God

Now hath conquered Death and Hell,
And bound the Devil who there doth dwell,
  So hath the Lord delivered Christendom;
  This was Christ himself:
                          Kyrie Eleison!

Fair Spring, thou dearest Season of the Year.

By CONRAD VON QUEINFURT, who died in Silesia in 1382. Miss WINKWORTH, who translates it, observes that it is quite in the style of the Minnesingers, both in thought and the carefully varied metre.

FAIR Spring, thou dearest season of
    the year,
  Thou art brimful of sweet delights:
The creatures robbed of joy by winter drear
  Thou dost repay for cold and gloomy nights.
    I feel thy airs are soft and mild;
    Thy winds are balmy, and not wild:
    Oh, how unlike the wintry blast!
    What Frost had bound in fetters fast
    Now feels the prison-time gone by;
      For 'tis unbound and free:
    Whether it climb or swim or fly,
      Whatever kind it be,
    Whether of water, earth, or sky,
      'Tis happy now we see.

The sun smiles with his lovely rays;
And sing, dear little birds, sing out your
    Maker's praise!

So many joys hath Spring; but most of all
  She hath one day above the rest,
That Christendom with one glad voice doth
    call
  Of all bright days the first and best.
    We hail thee, then, O chosen Day,
    With many a loud and gladsome lay.
    Thou art the day that God hath made:
    Well may our joy be now displayed!
    Thou art the Pascha to the Greek;
      And still we hear the Jew
    Of thee as Passover doth speak;
      And Latins know thee too
    As Transitus, that crowns the Holy
      Week:
But thou, where'er is heard the German
    tongue,
Art holy Easter-tide, when life from Death
    hath sprung.

We hail thee, blessed Day, we greet thee well,
  We praise thee ever, we adore
The Christ who triumphed over death and
    hell,
  Whose death slew Death forevermore.

O sweetest day, that saw'st Thee rise,
Our Paschal Lamb, our Sacrifice!
Our Brother, who hast won for us
A heritage most glorious!
Forest and foliage, corn and grass and flowers,
Would show their love to Thee!
The birds sing in the greening bowers:
Christ, they are praising Thee!
Thou wouldst not lack, had they our powers,
A song more worthy Thee!
For Thou art Conqueror, O Christ, to-day,
Who madest Death's great power itself give way!

So, Christians, triumph as your heart desires;
In chorus sweet and clear and strong,
Ye laymen in the church, ye priests in choirs,
Answer each other in your song.
Sing, "Christ the Lord is risen again;
Christ hath broken every chain."
The year of jubilee He bringeth in,
True freedom for all faithful hearts to win:
So to the table go thou solemnly,
Where in His flesh and blood
The Paschal Lamb itself is offered thee, —
The Lamb slain on the rood.

Praise the true Christ with happy hearts
    and free ;
  Praise Him, for He is good !
Thus, Spring, thou well may'st speak of joy to
    man :
Thou hast the Easter Day that ended Death's
    dark ban.

Christ the Lord is Risen Again!

An Easter hymn of the Bohemian Brethren in the fifteenth century. Translated into German by MICHAEL WEISS (died in 1540); and into English by CATHERINE WINKWORTH, in the second series of "Lyra Germanica." The Bohemian Brethren, according to Miss Winkworth (see "The Christian Singers of Germany"), were the remains of an ancient Slavonic Christianity, originating in the teaching of two Greek monks in the ninth century, and existing in Bohemia before the Papal authority and Roman liturgy found their way thither. They were among the first to hail the Reformation, and as early as 1522 offered Luther their co-operation. Their overtures, at first declined, were afterward accepted. They generally joined the Zwinglians, merging in that body, and thus disappearing from history, unless the United Brethren, or Moravians, may be regarded as an offshoot from them. Michael Weiss was born at Neisse, in Silesia. He was pastor of German-speaking congregations of Landskron and Fulnek, and for their benefit translated into German some of the finest Bohemian hymns, adding some of his own. His hymn-book was greatly admired by Luther, and passed through numerous editions in Germany and Holland.

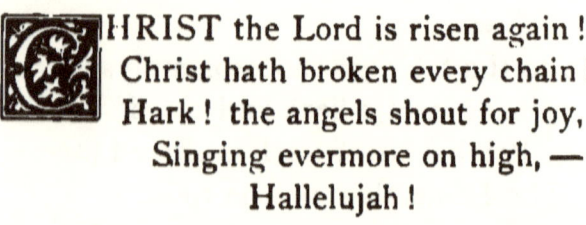

CHRIST the Lord is risen again !
Christ hath broken every chain !
Hark ! the angels shout for joy,
    Singing evermore on high, —
        Hallelujah !

He who gave for us His life,
Who for us endured the strife,
Is our Paschal Lamb to-day!
We, too, sing for joy, and say, —
      Hallelujah!

He who bore all pain and loss
Comfortless upon the cross
Lives in glory now on high,
Pleads for us, and hears our cry, —
      Hallelujah!

He whose path no records tell,
Who descended into hell,
Who the strong man armed hath bound,
Now in the highest heaven is crowned:
      Hallelujah!

He who slumbered in the grave
Is exalted now to save:
Now through Christendom it rings
That the Lamb is King of kings:
      Hallelujah!

Now He bids us tell abroad
How the lost may be restored;
How the penitent forgiven;
How we, too, may enter heaven:
      Hallelujah!

Thou, our Paschal Lamb indeed,
Christ, to-day Thy people feed;
Take our sins and guilt away:
Let us sing by night and day, —
    Hallelujah!

In the Bonds of Death He lay.

By Dr. MARTIN LUTHER, the great Reformer. He was born at Eisleben, Nov. 10, 1483; received his early education at Magdeburg, and Eisenach, where his progress was impeded by the poverty of his parents; entered the University of Erfurth in 1501, and graduated as Doctor of Philosophy with high honor. At the age of twenty-two he entered the Monastery of St. Augustine at Erfurth. In 1508 he became Professor of Philosophy in Wittenberg; and was soon afterward made Bachelor of Divinity, and appointed Chaplain to the Council of Wittenberg. During these years he had been passing through strong spiritual conflicts; and his close study of the Scriptures as a whole had given him new views of life and duty, and inspired his preaching with earnestness and power. His visit to Rome, with its revelation of the abuses of the Papacy; his encounter with Tetzel's doctrine of indulgences; his burning of the Papal bull in 1520; his summons to the Diet at Worms; his final rejection of monasticism in 1524, and marriage in 1525; and the wonderful work which he accomplished in establishing and extending the Protestant movement, by tongue and pen, by hymn and treatise, and translation of the Scriptures, — are matters too familiar to require recapitulation. His later years were years of comparative quiet, but of unceasing activity; and his death, on Feb. 18, 1546, was serene and jubilant. The following is based upon a Latin hymn of the fifteenth century: the translation into English is by Miss CATHERINE WINKWORTH.

IN the bonds of Death He lay
    Who for our offence was slain:
    But the Lord is risen to-day;
Christ hath brought us life again.

Wherefore let us all rejoice,
Singing loud with cheerful voice, —
   Hallelujah!

Of the sons of men was none
 Who could break the bonds of Death:
Sin this mischief dire had done;
 Innocent was none on earth:
Wherefore Death grew strong and bold,
Would all men in his prison hold:
   Hallelujah!

Jesus Christ, God's only Son,
 Came at last our foe to smite;
All our sins away hath done,
 Done away Death's power and right.
Only the form of Death is left;
Of his sting he is bereft:
   Hallelujah!

That was a wondrous war, I trow,
 When Life and Death together fought:
But Life hath triumphed o'er his foe;
 Death is mocked, and set at nought;
'Tis even as the Scripture saith, —
Christ through death has conquered Death:
   Hallelujah!

The rightful Paschal Lamb is He,
  On whom alone we all must live,
Who to death upon the tree
  Himself in wondrous love did give.
Faith strikes His blood upon the door;
Death sees, and dares not harm us more:
          Hallelujah!

Let us keep high festival
  On this most blessed day of days,
When God His mercy showed to all!
  Our Sun is risen with brightest rays,
And our dark hearts rejoice to see
Sin and night before Him flee:
          Hallelujah!

To the Supper of the Lord
  Gladly will we come to-day:
The word of peace is now restored,
  The old leaven is put away.
Christ will be our food alone;
Faith no life but His doth own:
          Hallelujah!

Ere yet the Dawn has filled the Skies.

By JOHANN HEERMAN, translated by Miss WINKWORTH. Heerman was born at Ranten, in Silesia, in 1585; and became early distinguished as a scholar, and a writer of Latin verses. He received the living of Köben, and retained it during the terrible suffering and devastation which the Thirty Years' War entailed upon Silesia. He was often in danger of his life from the Jesuits, and was several times compelled to flee; but in the midst of these troubled and tempestuous times he wrote and published three volumes of hymns, distinguished for earnestness, tenderness, and fervor. A large number of them have found a permanent place in German hymnology, and several have been translated into English. Worn out with conflict and sorrow, Heerman died in 1647.

ERE yet the dawn has filled the skies,
Behold my Saviour Christ arise!
He chaseth from us sin and night,
And brings us joy and life and light:
    Hallelujah! Hallelujah!

O stronger Thou than Death and Hell!
Where is the foe thou canst not quell?
What heavy stone Thou canst not roll
From off the prisoned, anguished soul?
    Hallelujah! Hallelujah!

If Jesus lives, can I be sad?
I know he loves me, and am glad!

Though all the world were dead to me,
Enough, O Christ, if I have Thee!
      Hallelujah! Hallelujah!

He feeds me, comforts and defends,
And, when I die, His angel sends
To bear me whither He is gone;
For of His own He loseth none:
      Hallelujah! Hallelujah!

No more to fear or grief I bow:
God and the angels love me now:
The joys prepared for me to-day
Drive fear and mourning far away:
      Hallelujah! Hallelujah!

Strong Champion! For this comfort see
The whole world brings her thanks to Thee;
And once we, too, shall raise above
More sweet and loud the song of love:
      Hallelujah! Hallelujah!

O Darkest Woe!

By JOHANN VON RIST, born near Hamburg in 1607; died in 1667. His father was a clergyman, and he was destined from the first for the study of theology. He was distinguished in his youth by precocious and varied talent; and when he returned to Hamburg, after study in the universities, and travel abroad, he had already acquired a reputation as a great scholar and poet. He was at once appointed to a church just outside Hamburg, and there spent the remainder of his life. He was an active pastor and a great preacher, a very strict Lutheran in doctrine, but more given to preaching against sin than against heresy. He published no less than ten collections of religious poems and hymns, containing between six hundred and seven hundred pieces. Many are of indifferent merit, but some belong to the first rank of hymns. He was crowned poet-laureate by the Emperor, and received a patent of nobility. Some of his contemporaries praised him as the Northern Apollo; and his hymns were eagerly caught up, and quickly adopted for congregational use in evangelical Germany. Even among Roman Catholics they were read with delight. The hymn which follows was written for Easter Eve. The translation is by Miss WINKWORTH.

DARKEST woe!
Ye tears, forth flow!
   Has earth so sad a wonder?
God the Father's only Son
   Now lies buried yonder.

  O son of man!
  It was the ban
Of death on thee that brought Him
  Down to suffer for thy sins,
And such woe hath wrought Him.

Behold, thy Lord,
   The Lamb of God,
Blood-sprinkled lies before thee,
   Pouring out His life, that He
May to life restore thee!

O ground of faith,
   Laid low in death!
Sweet lips now silent sleeping!
   Surely all that live must mourn
Here with bitter weeping.

Yea, blest is he
   Whose heart shall be
Fixed here; who apprehendeth
   Why the Lord of Glory thus
To the grave descendeth.

O Jesu blest,
   My help and rest!
With tears I pray, Lord, hear me:
   Make me love Thee to the last,
And in death be near me.

Jesus my Redeemer lives.

By LOUISA HENRIETTA, wife of the Elector of Brandenburg, born in 1628; died in 1677. She lived in a stormy and tragic time; but her character is one of the noblest examples of Christian womanhood that history presents. She was her husband's adviser in affairs of state, fostered agriculture by wise measures, founded primary schools all over the country, and won the love of her people by many acts of public and private charity. Many sweet and thoughtful hymns attest the depth and earnestness of her religious nature. That which follows ranks to this day among the most popular of German hymns. The translation is by Miss WINKWORTH. There is another translation, by Mrs. CHARLES, beginning, "Jesus, my eternal trust and my Saviour, ever liveth."

JESUS my Redeemer lives,
   Christ my trust is dead no more:
In the strength this knowledge gives,
   Shall not all my fears be o'er, —
Calm, though death's long night be fraught
Still with many an anxious thought?

Jesus my Redeemer lives,
   And His life I once shall see:
Bright the hope this promise gives, —
   Where He is, I too shall be.
Shall I fear, then? Can the Head
Rise, and leave the members dead?

Close to Him my soul is bound,
   In the bonds of Hope inclasped;
Faith's strong hand this hold hath found,
   And the Rock hath firmly grasped.
Death shall ne'er my soul remove
From her refuge in Thy love.

I shall see Him with these eyes, —
   Him whom I shall surely know;
Not another shall I rise:
   With His love this heart shall glow;
Only there shall disappear
Weakness in and round me here.

Ye who suffer, sigh, and moan,
   Fresh and glorious there shall reign:
Earthly here the seed is sown,
   Heavenly it shall rise again;
Natural here the death we die,
Spiritual our life on high.

Body, be thou of good cheer,
   In thy Saviour's care rejoice;
Give not place to gloom and fear:
   Dead, thou yet shalt know His voice,
When the final trump is heard,
And the deaf, cold grave is stirred.

Laugh to scorn, then, death and hell;
  Laugh to scorn the gloomy grave:
Caught into the air to dwell
  With the Lord who comes to save,
We shall trample on our foes,
Mortal weakness, fear, and woes.

Only see ye that your heart
  Rise betimes from earthly lust:
Would ye there with Him have part,
  Here obey your Lord, and trust;
Fix your hearts beyond the skies,
Whither ye yourselves would rise.

So Rest, my Rest.

By SOLOMON FRANK. Born at Weimar March 6, 1659: died June 11, 1725. He was the author of three hundred hymns, of which the following — one of seven Passion Hymns — is among the best. There is another translation, by Miss WINKWORTH, in "Lyra Germanica."

SO rest, my Rest,
  Forever blest,
    Thy grave with sinners making;
By Thy precious death from sin
  My dead soul awaking!

SO REST, MY REST.

Here hast Thou lain,
After much pain,
Life of my life, reposing:
Round Thee now a rock-hewn grave,
Rock of ages, closing.

Breath of all breath,
I know, from death,
Thou wilt my dust awaken:
Wherefore should I dread the grave,
Or my faith be shaken?

To me the tomb
Is but a room
Where I lie down on roses:
Who by death hath conquered death,
Sweetly there reposes.

The body dies
(Nought else), and lies
In dust, until victorious
From the grave it shall arise,
Beautiful and glorious.

Meantime I will,
My Jesus, still
Deep in my bosom lay Thee,
Musing on Thy death: in death
Be with me, I pray Thee.

O Risen Lord! O Conquering King!

By Dr. Justus H. Boehmer, a celebrated jurist, who was born at Hanover in 1674, and died at Halle in 1749. The translation is by Miss Catherine Winkworth, and is contained in the second series of the "Lyra Germanica."

O RISEN Lord! O conquering King!
    O Life of all that live!
    To-day that peace of Easter bring
Which only Thou canst give.
      Once Death, our foe,
      Had laid Thee low:
Now hast Thou rent his bonds in twain;
Now art Thou risen Who once was slain.

The power of Thy great majesty
    Bursts rocks and tombs away;
The victory raises us with Thee
    Into the glorious day:
      Now Satan's might
      And death's dark night
Have lost their power this blessed morn,
And we to higher life are born.

Oh that our hearts might inly know
    Thy victory over death,

And, gazing on Thy conflict, glow
  With eager, dauntless faith!
    Thy quenchless light,
    Thy glorious might,
Still comfortless and lonely leave
The soul that cannot yet believe.

Then break through our hard hearts Thy way,
  O Jesus, conquering King!
Kindle the lamp of faith to-day;
  Teach our faint hearts to sing
    For joy at length,
    That in Thy strength
We too may rise, whom sin had slain,
And Thine eternal rest attain.

And, when our tears for sin o'erflow,
  Do Thou in love draw near,
The precious gift of peace bestow,
  Shine on us bright and clear;
    That so may we,
    O Christ, from Thee
Drink in the life that cannot die,
And keep true Easter feasts on high.

Yes, let us truly know within
  Thy rising from the dead;

And quit the grave of death and sin;
And keep that gift, our Head,
That Thou didst leave
For all who cleave
To Thee through all this earthly strife:
So shall we enter into life.

O Glorious Head, Thou livest now!

By GERHARD TERSTEEGEN, born at Mors in Westphalia in 1697; died in 1769. He was the son of a tradesman, and, when a young man, supported himself for some years by weaving silk; leading meanwhile a life of meditation, and of almost entire seclusion from the world. Possessing a nature of singular spirituality and great benevolence, he was early led to undertake a kind of informal ministry, — laboring among the poor, addressing religious meetings, and publishing many hymns and devotional books. His health was always delicate, and he suffered many privations; but his life was long and useful, and he was greatly beloved He was a mystic of the purest type, and never connected himself with any religious sect. The following translation is by CATHERINE WINKWORTH.

O GLORIOUS Head, Thou livest now!
Let us Thy members share Thy life.
Canst Thou behold their need, nor bow
To raise Thy children from the strife
With self and sin, with death and dark distress,
That they may live to Thee in holiness?

Earth knows Thee not; but evermore
   Thou livest in Paradise, in peace:
Thither my soul would also soar;
   Let me from all the creatures cease:
Dead to the world, but to Thy Spirit known,
I live to Thee, O Prince of life, alone!

Break through my bonds, whate'er it cost;
   What is not Thine within me slay;
Give me the lot I covet most, —
   To rise as Thou hast risen to-day.
Nought can I do; a slave to death I pine:
Work Thou in me, O Power and Life Divine!

Work Thou in me, and heavenward guide
   My thoughts and wishes, that my heart
Waver no more, nor turn aside,
   But fix forever where Thou art:
Thou art not far from us: who love Thee well,
While yet on earth, in heaven with Thee may
      dwell.

Jesus Lives: no longer now.

By CHRISTIAN FURCHTEGOTT GELLERT, born in 1715, in Saxony; died in 1769. His father was a poet and a minister; and the son inherited from him a devout, religious nature, and rare poetical gifts. He taught and lectured upon Poetry and Eloquence, and is regarded as the head of a new didactic school of German hymn-writers. The translation is by FRANCES ELIZABETH COX, who, next to Miss Winkworth, is the most successful translator of German hymns.

JESUS lives: no longer now
    Can thy terrors, Death, appall me.
Jesus lives: by this I know,
    From the grave He will recall me.
Brighter scenes at death commence:
This shall be my confidence.

Jesus lives! to Him the throne
    High o'er heaven and earth is given:
I may go where He is gone,
    Live and reign with Him in Heaven.
God through Christ forgives offence:
This shall be my confidence.

Jesus lives! Who now despairs
    Spurns the Word which God hath spoken:

Grace to all that Word declares,
    Grace whereby sin's yoke is broken.
Christ rejects not penitence:
This shall be my confidence.

Jesus lives! for me He died:
    Hence will I, to Jesus living,
Pure in heart and act abide,
    Praise to Him, and glory, giving.
Freely God doth aid dispense:
This shall be my confidence.

Jesus lives! my heart knows well,
    Nought from me His Love shall sever;
Life, nor death, nor powers of hell,
    Part me now from Christ forever.
God will be a sure Defence:
This shall be my confidence.

Jesus lives! henceforth is death
    Entrance-gate of life immortal:
This shall calm my trembling breath
    When I pass its gloomy portal.
Faith shall cry, as fails each sense, —
Lord, Thou art my Confidence.

Rise again! yes, rise again wilt thou.

By Friedrich Gottlieb Klopstock, born at Quedlinburg in 1724; died in 1803. His is one of the greatest names in German literature. When a boy, he solemnly resolved that he would produce some great work that should do his country honor; and as early as the age of twenty-one he conceived the idea of his great epic, the "Messiah." In 1748, through solicitation of some friends, who by accident discovered the manuscript, the first three cantos of the "Messiah" were published; and these, with some odes printed at the same time, made him instantly famous throughout Germany. Seven cantos more were published before 1754; but domestic affliction interfered with the work, and for nine or ten years he published only minor religious poems. In 1773 the "Messiah" was at last completed, and in the same year a complete edition of his odes and lyrics was brought out. Klopstock was an ardent patriot, and a profound scholar; and the reverence paid to him in Germany was not unlike that enjoyed by Dr. Johnson in England. His character was singularly pure and amiable, and his bearing was marked by courtliness and dignity. His "Messiah" is a daring and sublime production, embracing an infinite variety of spectators and actors, and having its scene laid sometimes in the highest heaven. He wrote several scriptural dramas, and many odes, hymns, and lyrics. The following hymn is very commonly used at funerals or at Easter services. The translation is by Miss Winkworth. There is a more literal version by Alfred Baskerville, "Arise, yes, yes, arise again, O thou my dust!"

RISE again! yes, rise again wilt thou,
    My dust, though buried now!
        To life immortal
Is this brief rest the portal:
        Hallelujah!

For the seed is sown, again to bloom,
  Whene'er the Lord shall come,
    His harvest reaping
    In us who now are sleeping:
      Hallelujah!

Day of praise, of joyful tears the Day, —
  Thou of my God the Day, —
    When I shall number
    My destined years of slumber,
      Thou wakenest me!

Then shall we be like to those that dream,
  When on us breaks the beam
    Of that blest morrow:
    The weary pilgrim's sorrow
      Is then no more.

Then the Saviour leads us, of His grace,
  Into the Holiest Place,
    Where we forever
    Shall praise His name who doth deliver!
      Hallelujah!

Hallelujah! Jesus lives!

By CHRISTIAN GARVE, who was born at Breslau, Jan. 7, 1742; studied at Frankfort and Halle; in 1769 succeeded Gellert as Professor of Philosophy at Leipsic; and died Dec. 1, 1798. He was a man of amiable manners, and of good repute as a philosophical writer. From his very deathbed he dictated an essay on Patience. The translation which follows is by the compilers of " Hymns from the Land of Luther." These admirable volumes are the joint work of two sisters, Miss JANE BORTHWICK and Mrs. ERIC FINDLATER, who are descendants from an old Scottish family.

HALLELUJAH! Jesus lives!
 He is now the Living One.
From the gloomy house of death
 Forth the Conqueror has gone,
Bright forerunner to the skies
Of His people yet to rise.

Jesus lives! let all rejoice!
 Praise Him, ransomed ones of earth;
Praise Him, in a nobler song,
 Cherubim of heavenly birth;
Praise the Victor King, whose sway
Sin and death and hell obey.

Jesus lives! why weepest thou?
 Why that sad and frequent sigh?

He who died our Brother here
    Lives our Brother still on high, —
Lives forever, to bestow
Blessings on His Church below.

Jesus lives! and thus, my soul,
    Life eternal waits for thee:
Joined to Him, thy Living Head,
    Where He is, thou too shalt be;
With Himself, at His right hand,
Victor over death shalt stand.

Jesus lives! To Him my heart
    Draws with ever-new delight:
Earthly vanities, depart!
    Hinder not my heavenward flight!
Let this spirit ever rise
To its magnet in the skies.

Hallelujah! angels, sing;
    Join us in our hymn of praise;
Let your chorus swell the strain
    Which our feebler voices raise;
Glory to our God above,
And on earth His peace and love!

Christ hath Arisen!

By JOHANN WOLFGANG VON GOETHE, the greatest of German poets, born at Frankfort-on-the-Main in 1749; educated at Leipsic and Strasburg; died in March, 1832. His singularly active and fruitful mind was equally at home in literature and philosophy, in science and art; and the vast body of his published works might almost be said to constitute a literature in themselves. The following is the famous "Chorus of the Angels," from "Faust." The translation is by Rev. FREDERIC H. HEDGE, D.D., who was born in Cambridge, Dec. 12, 1805; graduated at Harvard College in 1825; was educated for the Unitarian ministry; filled pastorates at West Cambridge, Bangor, Providence, and Brookline; and since 1872 has held the Professorship of German Literature at Harvard. Bayard Taylor remarked of this chorus, that it is a stumbling-block to the translator, on account of the fivefold dactylic rhyme; and added, "Dr. Hedge, I believe, is the only one who has hitherto endeavored to reproduce the difficult structure of this chorus."

ANGELS.

HRIST hath arisen!
  Joy to our buried Head!
    Whom the unmerited,
Trailing inherited
  Woes, did imprison!

WOMEN.

Costly devices
  We had prepared, —
Shrouds and sweet spices,
  Linen and nard.

Woe the disaster!
   Whom we here laid,
Gone is the Master,
   Empty His bed.

ANGELS.

Christ hath arisen
Loving and glorious:
Out of laborious
Conflict victorious
   Christ hath arisen.

DISCIPLES.

Hath the inhumated,
   Upward aspiring,
Hath He consummated
   All His desiring?
Is He in benign bliss,
   Near to creative joy?
Wearily we in this
   Earthly house sigh;
Empty and hollow, us
   Left He unblest.
Master, Thy followers
   Envy Thy rest.

ANGELS.

Christ hath arisen
   Out of corruption's womb,
Burst every prison!
   Vanish death's gloom!
Active in charity,
Praise Him in verity!
His feast, prepare it ye!
His message, bear it ye!
His joy, declare it ye!
   Then is the Master near,
   Then is He here.

How brightly glows the Morning red!

Translated from the hymn-book of the Diocese of Trèves, by RICHARD FREDERICK LITTLEDALE.

OW brightly glows the morning red!
   Our Life hath conquered, Death hath fled.
The tomb is void, the warders foiled,
The Heavens exult, and hell is spoiled.
The whole creation's wide expanse
Joys in its risen Saviour's glance;

For He, Who dead and buried lay,
Hath cast the cords of death away.
His sacred wounds are gleaming bright,
And choirs of Angels in the height
Upon the clouds of purple rest,
To watch that resurrection blest.
Before the rising of the sun,
The women to the tomb are gone;
And store of spices with them bring,
To grace the Body of the King.
And lo! beside the open grave,
A white-robed Angel tidings gave, —
Why seek ye Him among the dead?
He hath arisen, and forth is sped.
Our eyes have seen, our tongues shall tell,
That Christ hath conquered death and hell;
The night of sin is done away,
And Judah's Lion wins the day.
Thy conquest is our faith. O Lord!
For evermore endures Thy word:
Believing thus, in hope we die,
To live in Thee for aye on high.

I say to all Men, Far and Near.

By FRIEDRICH VON HARDENBERG, better known by his literary pseudonyme of NOVALIS. He was born in Prussian Saxony in 1772, and studied at Leipsic and Wittenberg He wrote one or two romances, and a volume of hymns, and is characterized by Carlyle as "the most ideal of idealists" His literary activity was cut short by his early death, of consumption, March 19, 1801. The following translation is by Miss WINKWORTH.

I SAY to all men, far and near,
   That He is risen again;
That He is with us, now and here,
   And ever shall remain.

And what I say, let each this morn
   Go tell it to his friend, —
That soon in every place shall dawn
   His kingdom without end.

Now first to souls who thus awake
   Seems earth a fatherland :
A new and endless life they take
   With rapture from His hand.

The fears of death and of the grave
   Are whelmed beneath the sea;
And every heart, now light and brave,
   May face the things to be.

The way of darkness, that He trod,
  To heaven at last shall come;
And he who hearkens to His word
  Shall reach His Father's home.

Now let the mourner grieve no more,
  Though his beloved sleep:
A happier meeting shall restore
  Their light to eyes that weep.

Now every heart each noble deed
  With new resolve may dare:
A glorious harvest shall the seed
  In happier regions bear.

He lives: His presence hath not ceased,
  Though foes and fears be rife;
And thus we hail, in Easter's feast,
  A world renewed to life!

Sun, shine forth in all thy Splendor.

By C. J. P. Spitta, born at Hanover, Aug. 1, 1801; died Sept. 28, 1859. He was a graduate of the University of Göttingen, and a minister of the Lutheran Church. His character was marked by simplicity and gentleness, and his ministry was earnest and zealous. His hymns —, over one hundred in number — enjoy a great popularity in Germany. They have been translated into English by Mr. Richard Massie, in the "Lyra Domestica."

SUN, shine forth in all thy splendor;
    Joyfully pursue thy way:
For thy Lord and my Defender
    Rose triumphant on this day.
When He bowed His head, sore troubled,
    Thou didst hide thyself in night:
Shine forth now with rays redoubled;
    He is risen Who is thy light.

Earth, be joyous and glad-hearted;
    Spread out all thy vernal bloom:
For thy Lord is not departed;
    He has broken through the tomb.
When the Lord expired, wide-yawning,
    Thy strong rocks were rent with fright:
Greet thy risen Lord this morning,
    Bathed in floods of rosy light.

Say, my soul, what preparation
   Makest thou for this high day,
When the God of thy salvation
   Opened through the tomb a way?
Dwellest thou with pure affection
   On this proof of power and love?
Doth thy Saviour's resurrection
   Raise thy thoughts to things above?

Hast thou, borne on Faith's strong pinion,
   Risen with the risen Lord,
And, released from sin's dominion,
   Into purer regions soared?
Or art thou, in spite of warning,
   Dead in trespasses and sin?
Hath to thee the purple morning
   No true Easter ushered in?

Oh, then, let not death o'ertake thee
   By the shades of night o'erspread!
See! thy Lord has come to wake thee;
   He is risen from the dead.
While the time as yet allows thee,
   Hear: the gracious Saviour cries, —
"Sleeper, from thy sloth arouse thee;
   To new life at once arise!"

See, with looks of tender pity,
   He extends His wounded hands,

Bidding thee, with fond entreaty,
    Shake off sin's inthralling bands : —
"Wait not for some future meetness;
    Dread no punishment from me :
Rouse thyself, and taste the sweetness
    Of the new life offered thee."

Let no precious time be wasted;
    To new life arise at length :
He who death for thee hath tasted,
    For new life will give new strength.
Try to rise; at once bestir thee;
    Still press on, and persevere;
Let no weariness deter thee;
    He Who woke thee still is near.

Waste not so much time in weighing
    When and where thou shalt begin :
Too much thinking is delaying,
    Rivets but the chain of sin.
He will help thee, and provide thee
    With a courage not thine own,
Bear thee in His arms, and guide thee,
    Till thou learn'st to walk alone.

See! thy Lord Himself is risen,
    That thou mightest also rise,
And emerge from sin's dark prison
    To new life and open skies.

Come to Him who can unbind thee,
    And reverse thy awful doom;
Come to Him, and leave behind thee
    Thy old life, — an empty tomb!

Lamb, the Once Crucified!

By Mrs. Dr META HEUSSER-SCHWEIZER, whom Dr. Schaff ranks as the most gifted and sweetest of female poets in the German tongue. She was born in 1797 near Zurich, Switzerland, and in 1868 was still living there. The following sublime hymn was composed in 1831; and the translation — a singularly successful one — was contributed by Professor THOMAS C. PORTER of Lafayette College to Dr. Schaff's collection, "Christ in Song."

LAMB, the once crucified! Lion, by triumph surrounded!
    Victim all bloody, and Hero, who hell hast confounded!
Pain-riven Heart,
That from earth's deadliest smart
O'er all the heavens hast bounded! —

Thou in the depths wert to mortals the highest revealing,
God in humanity veiled, Thy full glory concealing!
    "Worthy art Thou!"
    Shouteth Eternity now,
Praise to Thee endlessly pealing.

Heavenly Love, in the language of earth past
    expression!
Lord of all worlds, unto whom every tongue
    owes confession!
  Didst Thou not go,
  And, under sentence of woe,
Rescue the doomed by transgression?

O'er the abyss of the grave, and its horrors
    infernal,
Victory's palm Thou art waving in triumph
    supernal:
  Who to Thee cling,
  Circled by hope, shall now bring
Out of its gulf life eternal.

Son of man, Saviour, in whom, with deep
    tenderness blending,
Infinite Pity to wretches her balm is extending,
  On Thy dear breast,
  Weary and numb, they may rest,
Quickened to joy never-ending.

Strange condescension! immaculate Purity,
    deigning
Union with souls where the vilest pollution
    is reigning,

Beareth their sin,
Seeketh the fallen to win,
Even the lowest regaining.

Sweetly persuasive, to me too Thy call has resounded,
Melting my heart so obdurate. Thy love has abounded:
Back to the fold,
Led by Thy hand, I behold
Grace all my path has surrounded.

Bless thou the Lord, O my soul! who, thy pardon assuring,
Heals thy diseases, and grants thee new life ever during;
Joy amid woe,
Peace amid strife here below,
Unto thee ever securing.

Upward, on pinions celestial, to regions of pleasure,
Into the land whose bright glories no mortal can measure,
Strong hope and love
Bear Thee, the fulness to prove
Of Thy salvation's rich treasure.

There, as He is, we shall view Him, with
    rapture abiding,
Cheered even here by His glance, when the
    darkness, dividing,
    Lets down a ray,
    O'er the perilous way
Thousands of wanderers guiding.

Join, O my voice! the vast chorus, with
    trembling emotion, —
Chorus of saints, who, though sundered by
    land and by ocean,
    With sweet accord
    Praise the same glorious Lord,
One in their ceaseless devotion.

Break forth, O Nature! in song, when the
    spring-tide is nighest;
World that hast seen His salvation, no longer
    thou sighest!
    Shout, starry train,
    From your empyreal plain, —
"Glory to God in the highest!"

The Lord of Life is Risen!

By Dr. JOHANN PETER LANGE, Professor at Bonn, and Editor of the well-known series of Bible Commentaries. He was born at Sonnborn April 10, 1802, and entered the University of Bonn in 1822. He became in 1841 Professor of Church History and Dogmatics at Zurich, and in 1854 Professor of Systematic Theology at Bonn, and in 1860 Counsellor of Consistory. The following translation is by the late Dr. HENRY HARBAUGH, of Mercersburg, Penn. (died Dec. 28, 1867), and was contributed to Dr. Schaff's "Christ in Song."

THE Lord of life is risen!
   Sing, Easter heralds! sing!
  He burst His rocky prison:
   Wide let the triumph ring.
Tell how the graves are quaking,
The saints their fetters breaking:
   Sing, heralds! Jesus lives!

In death no longer lying,
  He rose, the Prince, to-day:
Life of the dead and dying,
  He triumphed o'er decay.
The Lord of Life is risen:
In ruin lies Death's prison,
  Its keeper bound in chains.

We hear in Thy blest greeting, —
  Salvation's work is done!

THE LORD OF LIFE IS RISEN! 155

We worship Thee, repeating, —
  Life for the dead is won!
O Head of all believing!
O Joy of all the grieving!
  Unite us, Lord, to Thee.

Here at Thy tomb, O Jesus,
  How sweet the morning's breath!
We hear in all the breezes, —
  Where is thy sting, O Death?
Dark Hell flies in commotion;
While, far over earth and ocean,
  Loud Hallelujahs ring!

Oh, publish this salvation,
  Ye heralds, through the earth!
To every buried nation
  Proclaim the day of birth!
Till, rising from their slumbers,
The countless heathen numbers
  Shall hail the risen light.

Hail, hail, our Jesus risen!
  Sing, ransomed brethren, sing!
Through Death's dark, gloomy prison
  Let Easter chorals ring;
Haste, haste, ye captive legions!
Come forth from sin's dark regions;
  In Jesus' Kingdom live,

Up! sound your Joyful Songs victorious.

Translated from the German by HENRY THOMPSON, *and contributed to the* "Lyra Messianica."

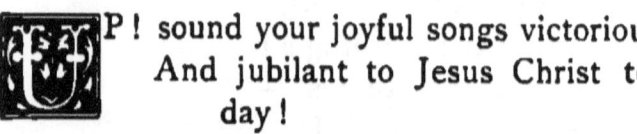P! sound your joyful songs victorious
    And jubilant to Jesus Christ to-day!
Back to His own he comes all-glorious :
    The grave's strong portals burst to make Him way.
He sank below, in pain and sore disgrace :
He mounts above, His pathway Angels trace.

Our God prevails! yes, fraud and malice
    Their little day may triumph o'er the Just :
God gives them back their poisoned chalice ;
    Our strength is He, our Helper and our Trust.
He gave indeed His Son to mortal pain :
This day He shows Him glorified again.

Praise, praise to him! the Lord is risen!
    Now is He Saviour, Lord, and God indeed ;
Redeemer from sin's deadly prison ;
    From death Redeemer, and from all our need.

The Father hath avouched Him His this day:
We reach our country through no other way.

Bliss, bliss, to us! now death hath o'er us
    No power to fright; to immortality,
Though Earth her veil may spread before us,
    Our spirits now are consecrate and free:
Could Christ arise thus potent from the grave,
His flock shall rise, whom thus He died to
    save.

From the Swedish.

Our Paschal Joy at Last is here!

Translated from the Swedish of LAURENCE PETERSEN, who wrote in the sixteenth century, by RICHARD FREDERICK LITTLEDALE, D. C. L. Dr. Littledale was born about 1830; graduated at Dublin University in 1855; was ordained deacon in 1856, and priest in 1857. He was curate in Thorpe Hamlet in 1856–7, and of St. Mary-the-Virgin, London, from 1857 to 1861. He has written several scholarly works in prose, chiefly on ecclesiastical subjects; was the principal editor of "The People's Hymnal;" and is the author of numerous excellent translations of Latin, Swedish, and German hymns.

OUR Paschal joy at last is here!
We praise Thee, Christ, Redeemer dear:
From death Thy servants Thou dost save,
Thyself arising from the grave.

The Tree of Life its Fruit hath borne, —
The Tree where Thou wast hung in scorn,
Whereon Thy rosy Blood was shed, —
And now we feed on Heavenly Bread.

We praise Thee, Jesu; for Thy hand
Hath freed us from corruption's band:

OUR PASCHAL JOY AT LAST IS HERE!

Our weary thraldom now is o'er;
We bow beneath the Law no more.

True Paschal Lamb, for sinners slain,
Christ, free from blemish, pure from stain,
Be Thou our Strength, our Food, our Life,
In all our need, in all our strife.

Thou Who hast conquered hell in fight,
We can do all things through Thy might, —
Set free the slaves to give Thee laud,
And bring them to the land of God.

O risen Lord! grant us to rise,
As Thou hast done, in joyful wise, —
First for Thy work, from error's gloom;
Then, on the last day, from the tomb.

We praise Thee, who from Death's fierce hold
The carnal, under evil sold,
Hast freed, and pointed out the way
Where we must tread to live for aye.

Dawn bursts o'er Death's Prison.

By Franz Michael Franzen, Bishop of Hörnösand, who was born at Uleaborg, Finland, in 1772, and died in 1847. He was educated at the University of Abo, and became professor of literary history there. Later he received the living of Kumla in Sweden, and in 1835 he became incumbent of Santa Clara in Stockholm. In 1841 he was appointed Bishop of Hörnösand. His poetry has been compared to that of the so-called Lake school of English poets, in its simple and accurate delineations of the natural, the domestic, and the idyllic. The following translation is by A. P. Hitchcock, one of the editors of "The Norwich (Conn.) Bulletin." The last three stanzas were first printed in a little Easter leaf-cluster called "Buona Pasqua," in 1878: the first two, completing the poem, were contributed by Mr. Hitchcock to a collection of Easter poetry, compiled by the editor of the present volume, which was published in "The Boston Journal" April 20, 1878.

DAWN bursts o'er Death's prison;
    Fulfilled is the Word!
To life He hath risen:
    Oh, joy to the Lord!
Redemption completed,
The last foe defeated,
The seal has been broken, the tomb is unbarred:
At the breath of His passing, in fright fled the guard,
And Tartarus groans, Alleluia!

    The darkness infernal
      Withstood Him in fight;

But victory eternal
  He won for the right.
Death's kingdom is ended:
  Faith rises again,
'Mid destinies blended,
  With Hope in her train.
Ye sorrowing women, why seek ye the dead?
From the grave He hath conquered, the Living hath fled!
  The Saviour hath risen, Alleluia!

Once more upon mortals
  God smileth in love:
The grave opes its portals
  To pathways above.
Heads bending in sadness
  'Neath Calvary's cross,
Look upward with gladness,
  Nor fear the world's loss!
Come back, scattered flock, to your Shepherd and Lord!
He liveth! He liveth! to watch you and ward,
  Unseen from the skies, Alleluia!

Ye ages, storm onward!
  His Church shall not fail:

As light spreads from sunward,
   His love shall prevail.
His messengers, flying
   Where foot hath e'er trod,
Through battling and dying,
   Bear witness of God, —
Bear witness of Thee, O Thou Trust in all
      need,
Who, dying for us, didst Thy followers lead
   Through death up to life, Alleluia!

Ye saints, why your sorrow,
   Your doubt and dismay?
The night and the morrow
   Will soon wear away.
Soon, soon in earth's bosom
   Shall sleep end your pain;
Soon life shall re-blossom
   And spring up like grain.
Himself, the great Sower, shall come at the
      end,
And winnow His wheat from the tares, and
      ascend
   To garner his sheaves, Alleluia!

English.

Done is a Battle on the Dragon Black.

By WILLIAM DUNBAR, who was born at Salton, in East Lothian, Scotland, about the year 1460. He took the degree of M.A., at St. Andrew's, in 1479, and was employed for some time as an itinerant or preaching friar. From about 1500 he lived chiefly about the court, and was the recipient of pensions and other tokens of royal favor. In 1511 he visited Scotland, in the train of Queen Margaret After the defeat at Flodden, and the king's death, his name disappears He is supposed to have died about 1520.' He had a wonderful variety of poetic gifts, as original as they were wide in range, and he may be fairly described as a Scotch Chaucer. His chief poems are "The Thistle and the Rose," and "The Golden Terge."

ONE is a battle on the Dragon black:
    Our Champion, Christ, confoundit
        has his force:
The yetts[1] of Hell are broken with a crack:
    The sign triumphal raist[2] is of the cross:
    The devils tremmils[3] with hideous voice:
The souls are borrowit,[4] and to the bliss can
    go:
    Christ with His blood our ransoms does indooce:[5]
Surrexit Dominus de sepulchro.

Dungin[6] is the deidly dragon Lucifer,
    The cruel serpent with the mortal stang;

[1] Gates. [2] Raised. [3] Trembles. [4] Redeemed. [5] Indorse.
[6] Overthrown. [7] Sting.

The auld keen tiger, with his teeth on char,[1]
    Whilk in a wait for us has lain so lang,
    Thinking to grip us in his clawis strang:
The merciful Lord would not that it were so;
    He made him to felye[2] of that fang:
Surrexit Dominus de sepulchro.

He for our sake that sufferit to be slain,
    And like a lamb in sacrifice was dicht,[3]
Is like a lion risen up again,
    And as gyane[4] has raxit[5] Him on hicht.
    Springin is Aurora radins and bricht,
On loft is gone the glorious Apollo,
    The blissful day departed fro the nicht:
Surrexit Dominus de sepulchro.

The great Victor again is risen on hicht,
    That for our quarrel to the death was woundit:
The sun that wox[6] all pale now shinis bricht,
    And darkness clear't, our faith is now refoundit:
    The knell of mercy fra the Heaven is soundit:
The Christians are deliverit of their wo,
    The Jewis and their error are confoundit:
Surrexit Dominus de sepulchro.

[1] On edge.   [2] Fail.   [3] Dressed.   [4] A giant.   [5] Raised.
[6] Waxed.

The foe is chas't, the battle is done ceiss,[1]
　　The prison broken, the jevellours fleet and
　　　　flemit:[2]
The war is gone, confirmit is the peiss,[3]
　　The fetters loosit, and the dungeon temit,[4]
　　The ransom maid, the prisoners redeemit:
The field is won, oure comin[5] is the fo,
　　Dispulit[6] of the treasure that he yemit:[7]
Surrexit Dominus de sepulchro.

[1] And ceased. [2] The jailers frightened and driven away.
[3] Peace. [4] Emptied. [5] Overcome. [6] Despoiled. [7] Prized.

Most Glorious Lord of Life! that on this Day.

By EDMUND SPENSER, who was born in London in 1553; graduated at Cambridge in 1572; died in London Jan. 15, 1599. He held several offices under the Crown, and resided for some years in Ireland, where at one time he possessed a large estate. By the breaking out o. rebellion he lost his property, and died in great destitution. "The Faery Queen" was his great work; but he wrote also many lesser pieces, and some exquisite sonnets. The following is the sixty-eighth of the "Amoreti."

MOST glorious Lord of Life! that on
　　this day
　　Didst make Thy triumph over death
　　　　and sin,
And, having harrowed hell, didst bring away
Captivity thence captive, us to win:
This joyous day, dear Lord, with joy begin;

And grant that we, for whom Thou diddest die,
Being with Thy dear blood clean washed from sin,
May live forever in felicity!
And that Thy love, we, weighing worthily,
May likewise love Thee for the same again;
And for Thy sake, that all like dear didst buy,
With love may one another entertain.
   So let us love, dear love, like as we ought:
   Love is the lesson which the Lord us taught.

Saviour of Mankind, Man! Emmanuel!

By GEORGE SANDYS, who was born at Bishopsthorpe, Yorkshire, in 1577, and died in March, 1643. He was a son of the Archbishop of York, and studied at Oxford. He made an extensive tour in Greece, Egypt, and the Holy Land, and published accounts of his travels, in prose and verse. After this, he became treasurer of the colony of Virginia, and, while in this country, published a translation of the Metamorphoses of Ovid, which was one of the earliest of American books. He published other works, in prose and verse; and Dryden styled him "the best versifier of the former age." The following lines, which are exquisitely finished, were written at the Temple of the Holy Sepulchre.

SAVIOUR of mankind, Man! Emmanuel!
   Who, sinless, died for sin; Who vanquished hell;

The first-fruits of the grave; Whose life did give
Light to our darkness; in Whose death we live:
Oh, strengthen Thou my faith, correct my will,
So that the latter death shall not devour
My soul sealed with Thy seal! So in the hour
When Thou, Whose body sanctified this tomb,
Unjustly judged, a glorious Judge shalt come
To judge the world with justice, by that sign
I shall be known and entertained for Thine.

Sleep, sleep, old Sun; thou canst not have re-past.

By Dr. JOHN DONNE, who was born in 1573, and died Dean of St. Paul's in 1631. He was educated for the law, but never practised it; and having lost his secretaryship to the Lord Chancellor Ellesmere through the revenge of Sir George More, whose daughter Donne had married in secret, he was for some years dependent on the generosity of his friends. He yielded only after prolonged reflection to the importunity of King James, who was so convinced of his fitness for the church that he would give him no other preferment. He was made Vicar of St. Dunstan's, and Dean of St. Paul's; and he gave himself up to his sacred duties with a whole-hearted devotion and sincerity which justified the king's estimate of his powers. Sorrow and poverty were not strangers to his life; but he preserved a serene and trustful spirit. He is usually considered as the first of the so-called "metaphysical poets" of the seventeenth century. There are many quaint, and some grotesque, conceits among his poems; but there is also considerable elevation of thought, and genuineness of feeling.

SLEEP, sleep, old sun; thou canst not
    have re-past [1]
As yet the wound thou took'st on
    Friday last.
Sleep, then, and rest: the world may bear
    thy stay;
A better sun rose before thee to-day;
Who, not content to enlighten all that dwell
On the earth's face, as thou, enlightened hell,
And made the dark fires languish in that vale,
As at thy presence here our fires grow pale;
Whose body, having walked on earth, and
    now

[1] Recovered.

Hastening to heaven, would, that He might allow
Himself unto all stations, and fill all,
For these three days become a mineral.
He was all gold when he lay down, but rose
All tincture; and doth not alone dispose
Leaden and iron wills to good, but is
Of power to make even sinful flesh like His.
Had one of those, whose credulous piety
Thought that a soul one might discern and see
Go from a body, at this sepulchre been,
And issuing from the sheet this body seen,
He would have justly thought this body a soul,
If not of any man, yet of the whole.

Let Faithfull Soules this Double Feast attend.

By Sir JOHN BEAUMONT, elder brother of Francis Beaumont the dramatist, born in 1582, and died in 1628. Among his writings are a few fine religious poems. The following was written upon the two great feasts of the Annunciation and the Resurrection, falling on the same day, March 25, 1627. Only the closing part is here given: the poem begins, "Thrice happy day, which sweetly dost combine."

LET faithfull soules this double feast attend
In two processions. Let the first descend

The temple's staires, and with a downe-cast
  eye
Vpon the lowest pavement prostrate lie:
In creeping violets, white lillies shine
Their humble thoughts, and ev'ry pure de-
  signe.
The other troope shall climbe with sacred
  heate
The rich degrees of Salomon's bright seate:
In glowing roses fervent zeale they beare;
And in the azure flowre-de-lis appeare
Celestial contemplations, which aspire
Above the skie, up to th' immortal quire.

Say, Earth, why hast thou got thee New Attire?

By GILES FLETCHER, the date of whose birth is by Chalmers conjectured to have been 1588; though it should probably be placed earlier, as the poet's "Canto" on the death of Elizabeth — a vigorous and mature production — was published in 1603. He graduated at Cambridge, studied theology, and was settled as Rector of Alderton, where he died in 1623. His chief work was "Christ's Victorie and Triumph," which was published in 1610, and is known to have had considerable influence in moulding the muse of Milton. The poem is now little read; but it contains some beautiful passages, which richly repay perusal. The following is taken from the fourth section of the poem, on "Christ's Triumph after Death." In the wide range of Easter poetry, there are few things more exquisite than this representation of the universal sympathy of Nature in the joy of the Resurrection. The text quoted is that of the edition of the Rev. Alexander B. Grosart, in the "Fuller Worthies' Library."

SAY, Earth, why hast thou got thee new attire,
   And stick'st thy habit full of dazies red?
Seems that thou doest to some high thought aspire,
And some newe-found-out bridegroome mean'st to wed.
Tell me, ye trees, so fresh appareèd,
   So neuer let the spitefull canker wast you,
   So neuer let the heau'ns with lightning blast you,
Why goe you now so trimly drest, or whither hast you?

Answer me, Iordan, why thy crooked tide
So often wanders from his neerest way,
As though some other way thy streame would
 slide,
And fain salute the place where something
 lay?
And you, sweete birds, that, shaded from the
 ray,
  Sit carrolling and piping griefe away,
  The while the lambs to heare you daunce
   and play, —
Tell me, sweete birds, what is it you faine
 would say?

And thou, fair spouse of Earth, that euerie
 yeare
Gett'st such a numerous issue of thy bride,
How chance thou hotter shin'st, and draw'st
 more neare?
Sure thou somewhear some worthie sight
 hast spide,
That in one place for ioy thou canst not bide.
  And you, dead swallowes, that so liuely now
  Through the flit [1] aire your winged passage
   rowe,
How could new life into your frozen ashes
 flowe?

[1] Flitting; i.e., moving.

Ye primroses and purple violets,
Tell me, why blaze ye from your leauie[1] bed,
And wooe men's hands to rent you from your sets,
As though you would somewhear be carrièd,
With fresh perfumes and velvets garnishèd?
  But ah! I neede not aske, 'tis surely so;
  You all would to your Sauiour's triumphs goe:
There would ye all waaite and humble homage doe.

Thear should the Earth herselfe, with garlands newe
And louely flow'rs embellishèd, adore:
Such roses neuer in her garland grewe,
Such lillies neuer in her brest she wore,
Like beautie neuer yet did shine before:
  Thear should the sunne another sunne behold,
  From whence himselfe borrowes his locks of gold,
That kindle heau'n and earth with beauties manifold.

There might the violet and primrose sweet,
Beames of more liuely and more louely grace,

[1] Leafy.

Arising from their beds of incense meet ;
Thear should the swallows see new life em-
    brace
Dead ashes, and the graue vnheal [1] his face,
  To let the living from his bowels creepe,
  Vnable longer his owne dead to keepe :
There heau'n and earth should see their Lord
    awake from sleepe.

[1] Unveil, or uncover.

This is the Day the Lord hath made.

By GEORGE WITHER, born at Bentworth, Hampshire, in 1588; died 1667. He graduated at Oxford, and studied law, but soon adopted literature as a profession. His life was a troubled one, and he was twice imprisoned for political writings. He was a captain of horse in an expedition against the Scots in 1639, but on the rise of the Commonwealth raised a troop of horse for the Parliament, and won the rank of major. He was a man of deep and fervid convictions. He was a voluminous writer. His poetry abounds in forced and fanciful conceits, and much of it is on trivial themes; but it contains many gems which were not adequately appreciated during the poet's lifetime, nor for several generations after.

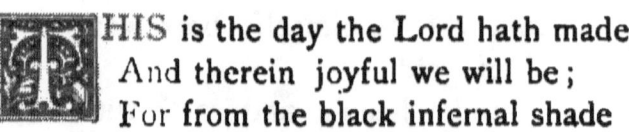HIS is the day the Lord hath made,
  And therein joyful we will be ;
For from the black infernal shade
In triumph back returned is He :
The snares of Satan and of Death
He hath victoriously undone,
And fast in chains He bound them hath,
His triumph to attend upon.

The grave, which all men did detest,
And held a dungeon full of fear,
Is now become a bed of rest,
And no such terrors find we there.
For Jesus Christ hath took away
The horror of that loathed pit;
E'en ever since that glorious day
In which Himself came out of it.

His mockings, and His bitter smarts,.
He to our praise and ease doth turn;
And all things to our joy converts,
Which He with heavy heart hath borne:
His broken flesh is now our food;
His blood is shed, is ever since
That drink which doth our souls most good,
And that which shall our foulness cleanse.

Those wounds so deep, and torn so wide,
As in a rock our shelters are;
That which they pierced through His side
Is made a dove-hole for His dear:
Yea, now we know, as was foretold,
His flesh did no corruption see;
And that hell wanted strength to hold
So strong and one so blest as He.

Oh! let us praise His name therefore,
(Who thus the upper hand hath won,)

For we had else, forevermore,
Been lost and utterly undone:
Whereas His favor doth allow
That we with boldness thus may sing:—
O Hell! where is thy conquest now?
And thou (O Death)! where is thy sting?

Hence they have Born my Lord. Behold! the Stone.

By ROBERT HERRICK, who was born in 1591, and died about 1674. He studied for a time at Cambridge, with the intention of adopting the legal profession; but changed his purpose, and entered into holy orders. From 1629 to 1648 he was Vicar of Dean Prior in Devonshire, but was ejected by the Puritan party, to whom his royalism and his loose morals were alike distasteful. He lived for some years in London, so poor as to be a recipient of charity, but enjoying converse with the literary wits of the day. About 1660 his vicarage was restored to him, and he retained it until his death. He was ill adapted to the sacred office, and his verse exhibits the same fluctuations and contradictions as his life. The following is found among his "Noble Numbers."

HENCE they have born my Lord.
    Behold! the stone
Is rowl'd away, and my sweet Sav-
    iour's gone.
Tell me, white angell, what is now become
Of Him we lately seal'd up in this tombe?
Is He from hence gone to the shades beneath
To vanquish Hell, as here He conquer'd
    Death?
If so, I'le thither follow without feare,
And live in hell, if that my Christ stayes there.

Rise, Heart: thy Lord is Risen. Sing His Praise.

By GEORGE HERBERT, who, by reason of his saintly life and devout poetry, came to be known as "holy George Herbert." He was born at Montgomery Castle, Wales, April 3, 1593; graduated with high honors at Cambridge, and became a fellow of Trinity College in 1615. He took orders, and became prebendary of Leighton Bromswold, in 1626; was married in 1630; and was given the living of Bemerton, near Salisbury, where he died in February, 1632. In 1631 he published "The Temple: Sacred Poems and Private Ejaculations:" and several volumes of his writings, in prose and verse, were published after his death.

RISE, heart: thy Lord is risen. Sing
    His praise,
        Without delayes,
Who takes thee by the hand, that thou likewise
    With Him may'st rise;
That, as His death calcined thee to dust,
His life may make thee gold, and much more just.

Awake, my lute, and struggle for thy part
    With all thy art:
The crosse taught all wood to resound His name
    Who bore the same;
His stretched sinews taught all strings what key
Is best to celebrate this most high day.

RISE, HEART: THY LORD IS RISEN.

Consort, both heart and lute, and twist a song
        Pleasant and long:
Or, since all musick is but three parts vied,
        And multiplied,
Oh, let thy blessed Spirit bear a part,
And make up our defects with His sweet art!

I got me flowers to straw Thy way;
I got me boughs off many a tree:
But Thou wast up by break of day,
And brought'st Thy sweets along with Thee.

The Sunne arising in the East,
Though he give light, and th' East perfume,
If they should offer to contest
With Thy arising, they presume.

Can there be any day but this,
Though many sunnes to shine endeavor?
We count three hundred; but we misse:
There is but one, and that one ever.

Lord, who createdst Man in Wealth and Store.

By GEORGE HERBERT, 1593-1632. See note to the preceding hymn. The title is "Easter-Wings," and the fanciful construction of the verse is in accord with the thought.

LORD, who createdst man in wealth and store,
Though foolishly he lost the same,
Decaying more and more,
Till he became
Most poor;

With Thee,
Oh, let me rise,
As larks, harmoniously,
And sing this day Thy victories;
Then shall the fall further the flight in me.

My tender age in sorrow did beginne;
And still with sicknesses and shame
Thou didst so punish sinne,
That I became
Most thinne.

With Thee
Let me combine,
And feel this day Thy victorie;
For, if I imp my wing on thine,
Affliction shall advance the flight in me.

Alas, Poore Death! where is thy Glorie?

By GEORGE HERBERT, 1593-1632. It is entitled "A Dialogue-Anthem," and Christian and Death are the speakers.

CHRISTIAN.

LAS, poore Death! where is thy glorie?
Where is thy famous force, thy ancient sting?

DEATH.

Alas, poore mortall, void of storie,
Go spell and reade how I have killed thy King.

CHRISTIAN.

Poore Death! and who was hurt thereby?
Thy curse being laid on Him makes thee accurst.

DEATH.

Let losers talk, yet thou shalt die:
These arms shall crush thee —

CHRISTIAN.

Spare not; do thy worst:
I shall be one day better than before;
Thou so much worse, that thou shalt be no more.

Death, thou wast once an Uncouth Hideous Thing.

By George Herbert, 1593–1632.

DEATH, thou wast once an uncouth
      hideous thing,
         Nothing but bones;
   The sad effect of sadder grones :
Thy mouth was open, but thou couldst not sing.

For we consider'd thee as at some six
         Or ten yeares hence,
   After the losse of life and sense,
Flesh being turn'd to dust, and bones to
      sticks.

We lookt on this side of thee, shooting short;
         Where we did finde
   The shells of fledge souls left behinde,
Dry dust, which sheds no tears, but may
      extort.

But since our Saviour's death did put some
      bloud
         Into thy face,
   Thou art grown fair and full of grace,
Much in request, much sought for, as a good.

For we do now behold thee gay and glad
   As at doomsday,
 When souls shall wear their new aray,
And all thy bones with beautie shall be clad.

Therefore we can go die as sleep, and trust,
   Half that we have,
Unto an honest, faithfull grave;
Making our pillows either down, or dust.

Up, and Away!

 By CHRISTOPHER HARVEY, who was born at Bunbury, in Cheshire, in 1597; graduated at Brasen-nose College in 1613; took holy orders, and was made Vicar of Clifton. He wrote and published anonymously, in 1647, "The Synagogue," a series of poems in close imitation of George Herbert; and the work is frequently affixed to Herbert's poems. He died April 1, 1663. The following is taken from "The Synagogue," as contained in Grosart's "Fuller Worthies Library."

UP, and away!
  Thy Saviour's gone before:
 Why dost thou stay,
  Dull soul? Behold, the door
Is open, and His precept bids thee rise,
Whose pow'r hath vanquish't all thine ene-
   mies.
Say not, I live,
  Whilst in the grave thou ly'st:
He that doth give
  Thee life would have thee prize't

More highly than to keep it buri'd where
Thou canst not make the fruits of it appear.
Is rottenness
    And dust so pleasant to thee,
That happiness
    And heaven cannot woo thee
To shake thy shackles off, and leave behind
    thee
Those fetters, which to death and hell do
    bind thee?
In vain thou say'st
    Thou'rt bury'd with thy Saviour,
If thou delay'st
    To shew by thy behaviour
That thou art risen with Him. Till thou shine
Like Him, how canst thou say His light is
    thine?
Early He rose,
    And with Him brought the day,
Which all thy foes
    Frighted out of the way;
And wilt thou sluggard-like turn in thy bed,
Till noon-sun beams draw up thy drowsy
    head?
Open thine eyes,
    Sin-seisèd soul, and see
What cobweb-tyes
    They are that trammel thee;

Not profits, pleasures, honors, as thou thinkest,
But loss, pain, shame, at which thou vainly
    winkest.
All that is good
    Thy Saviour dearly bought
With His heart's blood ;
    And it must there be sought,
Where He keeps residence Who rose this
    day.
Linger no longer, then : up, and away !

What Faithless, Froward, Sinful Man.

The following ballad is contained in the Roxburghe Collection, and its date is between 1560 and 1700. It was printed as a broadside, in black-letter, under the title, "A most Godly and Comfortable Ballad of the Glorious Resurrection of our Lord Jesus Christ, how He triumphed over Death, Hell, and Sin, whereby we are certainly persuaded of our rising again from the Dead." Below the title was a rude wood-cut. In this Christ appears on a bow among opening clouds. On either side, at His feet, angels blow trumpets. In the centre foreground stands the cross, before which a miscellaneous company kneel; while beyond it the dead are rising from their graves in their shrouds. The ballad claims attention less by its poetic qualities than by the simplicity and directness with which it recites the incidents of the Resurrection.

WHAT faithless, froward, sinful man
    so far from grace is fled,
That doth not in his heart believe
    the Rising of the Dead ?
Or why do wicked mortal men
    their lives so vainly frame,

That, being Dead, they do suppose
   they shall not rise again?

For why, if that the Dead indeed,
   which now consuming lyes,
Shall not by God be rais'd again,
   then Christ did never rise:
And if so be our Saviour sweet
   he did not rise from death,
Our Preaching is of no effect,
   and vain's our hope on Earth.

If Christ rose not, again I say,
   then are we yet in sin,
And they that fall asleep in him
   no part of joy shall win.
Of all the creatures living, then,
   which God on earth did frame,
Most wretched are the states of men
   which spend their days in vain.

But Christ is risen up from Death,
   as it was right and meet,
And thereby trod down Death and Hell
   and sin under His feet;
And, that the same to sinful men
   the plainer might appear,
The glorious rising of the Lord
   his word declareth clear.

When he within the grave was laid,
   the Jews did Watch-men set,
Lest by his friends his corp thence
   should secretly be fet :
A mighty Stone likewise they did
   on his Sepulchre role,
And all for fear his body should
   away from thence be stole.

But in the Dead time of the night
   a mighty earth-quake came,
The which did shake both Sea and Land,
   and all within the same ;
And then the Angel of the Lord
   came down from Heaven so high,
And rol'd away the mighty stone
   which on the ground did lie.

His face did shine like flaming fire,
   his Cloathes were white as snow,
Which put the watchmen in great fear,
   who ran away for woe,
And told unto the High-Priest, plain,
   what I do now rehearse ;
Who hired them for money straight,
   that they should hold their peace.

And say, quoth he, his servants came,
   whom he sometimes did keep,

And secretly stole him away,
  while ye were fast asleep;
And, if that Herod hear thereof,
  we will persuade him so,
That you shall find no hurt at all
  wherever you do go.

But faithful Mary Magdalen,
  and James her Brother too,
They brought great store of Oyntment,
  as Jewes were wont to do;
Who rose up early in the morn,
  before that it was day,
The body of the Lord t'annoint
  in grave whereas he lay.

And when unto the Grave they came,
  they were in wondrous fear:
They saw a young man in the same;
  but Christ they saw not there.
Then said the Angel unto them,
  why are you so afraid?
The Lord, whom you do seek, I know
  is risen up, he said.

Then went these women both away,
  who told these tidings than
To John and Peter, who in haste
  to the Sepulchre ran;

Who found it as the woman said,
  and then away did go;
But Mary stayed, weeping still,
  whose tears declar'd her woe;

Who, looking down into the grave,
  two Angels there did see:
Qd they, Why weeps this woman so?
  even for my Lord, Qd she;
And turning then herself about,
  as she stood weeping so,
The Lord was standing at her back;
  but him she did not know.

Why doth this woman weep? he said:
  whom seek'st thou in this place?
She thought it had the gard'ner been;
  and thus she shows her case:
If thou hast borne him hence, she said,
  then tell me where he is;
And for to fetch him back again
  be sure I will not miss.

What, Mary! then our Saviour said,
  dost thou lament for me?
O Master, livest Thou again?
  My soul doth joy in thee!
O Mary, touch me not, He said,
  ere I have been above,

Even with my God, the only God
  and Father whom we love.

And oftentimes did Christ appear
  to his Disciples all:
Yet Thomas would not it believe,
  his faith it was so small,
Except that he might thrust his hand
  into the wound so wide,
And put his finger where the spear
  did pierce the tender side.

Then Christ, which knew all secrets,
  to them again came he,
Who said to Thomas, Here I am;
  as plainly thou may'st see.
See here the hands which nails did pierce,
  and holes are in my side;
And be not faithless, O thou man
  for whom these pains I bide!

Thus sundry times he shew'd himself
  when he did rise again,
And then ascended into Heaven,
  in glory for to reign;
Where he prepares a place for those
  whom he shall raise likewise,
To live with him in Heavenly bliss,
  above the lofty skies.

What Glorious Light!

By JEREMY TAYLOR, D.D., who was born at Cambridge 1613: and died at Lisburn Aug. 13, 1667. He was the son of a barber; but his father, who had been in better circumstances, did his utmost to advance his education. He graduated at Caius College in 1631, was ordained in 1633, and, after continuing his studies for a time at Oxford, was appointed to the fellowship at All Souls. He served as rector of Uppingham, Rutlandshire, and as chaplain of Charles I. at Oxford. He kept a school at Llanvihangel in Carmarthenshire, and there wrote some of his greatest works. He was taken prisoner at the siege of the Castle of Cardigan. In 1660 he signed the declaration of the Royalists, and won the notice of the restored king, Charles II., who made him Bishop of Down, Connor, and Dromore, and Vice-Chancellor of the University of Dublin. He published a number of theological works, volumes of sermons, &c., and is now best known by his "Rules for Holy Living and Dying." His style is rich, quaint, and learned, with some marked defects as well as excellences, — at once rewarding study and discouraging imitation. The following is one of his "Festival Hymns" appended to the "Golden Grove," a manual of prayers.

HAT glorious light!
    How bright a sun, after so sad a
        night,
Does now begin to dawn! Bless'd were those
        eyes
  That did behold
  This Sun, when he did first unfold
    His glorious beams, and now begin to rise.
It was the holy tender sex
  That saw the first ray:
St. Peter and the other had the reflex,
  The second glimpse o' th' day.

Innocence had the first ; and he
That fled, and then did penance, next did see
  The glorious Sun of righteousness
    In his new dress
Of triumph, immortality, and bliss.
O dearest God, preserve our souls
    In holy innocence!
Make us to rise again to th' life of grace;
That we may live with thee, and see Thy
    glorious face,
  The crown of holy penitence.

Rise, Heir of Fresh Eternity.

BY RICHARD CRASHAW, who was born in London about 1616; graduated at Cambridge, where he obtained a fellowship in 1637; and entered the English Church in 1641, becoming an earnest and eloquent preacher. The Parliament ejected him from his fellowship in 1644 for refusing to take the Covenant, and he soon after adopted the Roman-Catholic faith. After some hardships, he was recommended to certain Italian dignitaries. He was appointed secretary to one of the cardinals, and canon of the Church of Lorette In this office he died in 1650. He wrote both Latin and English poems; and the latter, of which the following is a good example, greatly resemble the hymns of George Herbert.

RISE, heir of fresh eternity,
  From thy virgin-tomb ;
Rise, mighty man of wonders, and
  thy world with thee ;
Thy tomb, the universal East, —
  Nature's new womb ;
Thy tomb, — fair Immortality's perfumèd nest.

Of all the glories¹ make noon gay
   This is the morn;
This rock buds forth the fountain of the
      streams of day;
   In joy's white annals lives this hour,
     When life was born,
No cloud-scowl on his radiant lids, no tempest-lower.

   Life, by this light's nativity,
     All creatures have;
Death only by this day's just doom is forced
      to die.
   Nor is Death forced; for, may he lie
     Throned in thy grave,
Death will on this condition be content to die.

[1] *Which* understood.

Death and Darkness, get You packing!

By HENRY VAUGHN, born in Newton, Wales, in 1621; and died April 23, 1695. He studied at Oxford, and became a physician; but chiefly delighted in literary pursuits. He was an admirer and disciple of Herbert; and his "Silex Scintillans," a collection of sacred poems, was modelled after Herbert's "Temple." His earlier poetry was of a secular order, although free from the objectionable features of the poetry of the time. Severe illness gave a more serious turn to his mind; and he wrote several devotional works in prose, besides the volume of sacred poems already referred to. He associated with men of genius in London; but his poetry was not appreciated during his life. It exhibits the defects as well as the excellences of its model; but is quaint, striking, suggestive, and very often impressive.

DEATH and darkness, get you packing!
Nothing now to man is lacking;
All your triumphs now are ended,
And what Adam marr'd is mended.
Graves are beds now for the weary,
Death a nap to wake more merry;
Youth now, full of pious duty,
Seeks in thee for perfect beauty;
The weak and aged, tired with length
Of daies, from thee look for new strength;
And infants with thy pangs contest
As pleasant as if with the brest.
Then unto Him who thus hath thrown
Even to contempt thy kingdome down,

And by His blood did us advance
Unto His own inheritance,
To Him be glory, power, praise,
From this unto the last of daies!

Thou Whose sad Heart and Weeping Head lyes Low.

By HENRY VAUGHN, 1621-1695. — See note to preceding.

THOU whose sad heart and weeping
head lyes low,
  Whose cloudy brest cold damps invade,
Who never feel'st the sun, nor smooth'st thy
brow,
  But sitt'st oppressed in the shade, —
                     Awake! awake!
And in His resurrection partake,
Who on this day, that thou might'st rise as He,
Rose up, and cancell'd two deaths due to thee.

Awake! awake! and, like the sun, disperse
  All mists that would usurp this day:
Where are thy palms, thy branches, and thy
verse?
  Hosanna! hark! why dost thou stay?
                     Arise! arise!

And with his healing bloud anoint thine eyes,
Thy inward eyes: His bloud will cure thy
    mind,
Whose spittle only could restore the blind.

Blest Morning, whose Young Dawning Rays.

By ISAAC WATTS, D.D., one of the most famous and prolific of English hymn-writers. He was born at Southampton July 17, 1674; and died Nov. 25, 1748. He possessed such precocious talents, that he began the study of Latin in his fourth year, and wrote very tolerable hymns at the age of seven. He was a minister of the Independent Church in London, and he wrote in prose as well as verse, — his best-known prose work being a treatise on Logic and Improvement of the Mind.

BLEST morning, whose young dawning
    rays
  Beheld our rising God;
That saw Him triumph o'er the dust,
  And leave His dark abode!

In the cold prison of a tomb
  The dead Redeemer lay,
Till the revolving skies had brought
  The third, the appointed day.

Hell and the grave unite their force
  To hold our God in vain:
The sleeping Conqueror arose,
  And burst their feeble chain.

To Thy great name, Almighty Lord,
  These sacred hours we pay,
And loud hosannas shall proclaim
  The triumph of the day.

Salvation and immortal praise
  To our victorious King!
Let heaven and earth, and rocks and seas,
  With glad hosannas ring!

Yes, the Redeemer rose.

By PHILIP DODDRIDGE, D.D., who was born in London in 1702, and died at Lisbon in 1751. He was pastor of a Congregational church at Kibworth, and later at Northampton, where he also carried on an academy. Here two hundred students received their training, of whom one hundred and twenty entered the ministry. He was a man of rare piety and industry, and occupied a sphere of wide usefulness as pastor, preacher, teacher, expositor of the Scriptures, and author of religious works in prose and verse. His hymns were written to be sung at the close of his sermons; and they have been compared to "spiritual amber, fetched up and floated off from sermons long since lost in the depths of bygone time." They were published after his death. He was never of robust health, and his multiplied labors hastened the pulmonary disease which caused his death.

YES, the Redeemer rose:
  The Saviour left the dead,
And o'er our hellish foes
  High raised His conquering head.
    In wild dismay,
    The guards around
    Fell to the ground,
    And sunk away.

Lo! the angelic bands
  In full assembly meet,
To wait His high commands,
  And worship at His feet:
    Joyful they come,
    And wing their way
    From realms of day
    To such a tomb.

Then back to heaven they fly,
  And the glad tidings bear:
Hark! as they soar on high,
  What music fills the air!
    Their anthems say, —
    "Jesus, Who bled,
    Hath left the dead:
    He rose to-day."

Ye mortals, catch the sound,
  Redeemed by Him from hell,
And send the echo round
  The globe on which you dwell:
    Transported, cry, —
    "Jesus, Who bled,
    Hath left the dead,
    No more to die."

All hail, triumphant Lord,
  Who sav'st us with Thy blood!
Wide be Thy name adored,
  Thou rising, reigning God!
    With Thee we rise,
    With Thee we reign,
    And empires gain
    Beyond the skies.

Christ the Lord is risen To-day.

By CHARLES WESLEY, one of the founders of Methodism, and one of the sweetest, as he was certainly the most prolific, of English hymn-writers. He was born at Epworth Dec. 18, 1708, and graduated at Oxford. In 1735 he took orders, and immediately went to Georgia as a missionary, in company with his brother John. The mission was unsuccessful; but its results were of great importance to the Wesleys, as their intercourse with the Moravian Christians who sailed in the same ship with them led them to embrace their views. On their return to England they formed, in conjunction with Whitefield and others, the first Methodist society, in Fetter Lane, London; and thenceforth their lives were devoted to propagating the doctrines and illustrating the principles of that zealous and active denomination. Charles Wesley died March 29, 1788, leaving behind him more than four thousand published hymns, and over two thousand in manuscript. In such a vast body of verse there must needs be much chaff; but there are also many grains of pure wheat.

CHRIST the Lord is risen to-day,
  Sons of men, and angels, say:
  Raise your joys and triumphs high;
Sing, ye heavens; and, earth, reply.

Love's redeeming work is done,
Fought the fight, the battle won :
Lo! our Sun's eclipse is o'er ;
Lo! He sets in blood no more.

Vain the stone, the watch, the seal :
Christ hath burst the gates of hell!
Death in vain forbids His rise :
Christ hath opened Paradise!

Lives again our glorious King :
Where, O Death, is now thy sting?
Once He died our souls to save :
Where thy victory, O grave?

Soar we now where Christ has led,
Following our exalted Head.
Made like Him, like Him we rise :
Ours the cross, the grave, the skies.

What though once we perished all,
Partners in our parents' fall?
Second life we all receive,
In our Heavenly Adam live.

Risen with Him, we upward move :
Still we seek the things above ;
Still pursue, and kiss the Son,
Seated on His Father's throne.

Scarce on earth a thought bestow,
Dead to all we leave below:
Heaven our aim, and loved abode;
Hid our life with Christ in God, —

Hid till Christ our Life appear,
Glorious in His members here:
Joined to Him, we then shall shine,
All immortal, all divine.

Hail the Lord of earth and heaven!
Praise to Thee by both be given!
Thee we greet triumphant now:
Hail, the Resurrection Thou!

King of glory, Soul of bliss!
Everlasting life is this,
Thee to know, Thy power to prove,
Thus to sing, and thus to love!

Mary to her Saviour's Tomb.

By JOHN NEWTON, who was born in London in 1725, and died Dec. 21, 1807. His early life was wild and romantic. He was an infidel and a profligate. He devoted himself to a seafaring life; and it was on his voyage home from Africa — where he had lived in the service of a slave-trader — in 1748, during a terrific storm, that the truth of Christianity broke in upon him, and he became a changed man. For some years he continued to follow the sea; but in 1758 he began to preach, and, after six years of study, entered upon a regular ministry in the curacy of Olney. In 1779 he became rector of a London church, and his labors were earnest and fruitful. He published several volumes in prose, and was the principal author of the Olney Hymns.

MARY to her Saviour's tomb
    Hasted at the early dawn:
Spice she brought, and sweet perfume;
    But the Lord she loved was gone.
For a while she weeping stood,
    Struck with horror and surprise;
Shedding tears, a plenteous flood,
    For her heart supplied her eyes.

Grief and sighing quickly fled
    When she heard His welcome voice:
Just before, she thought Him dead;
    Now He bids her heart rejoice.
What a change His word can make,
    Turning darkness into day!

You who weep for Jesus' sake,
  He will wipe your tears away.

He who came to comfort her
  When she thought her all was lost
Will for your relief appear,
  Though you now are tempest-tossed.
On His word your burden cast,
  On His love your thoughts employ:
Weeping for a while may last;
  But the morning brings the joy.

The Happy Morn is come!

By THOMAS HAWEIS, LL.B., born at Truro, Cornwall, in 1732; died in 1820. He graduated at Christ's College, Cambridge, and held a rectorship at Aldwinkle, Northamptonshire. He was a popular preacher, and one of the founders of the London Missionary Society. He was the author of several prose works, — among them a translation of the New Testament, and a commentary on the Bible, — and of a volume of hymns entitled "Carmina Christo."

THE happy morn is come!
    Triumphant from the grave,
  The Lord hath left the tomb,
    Omnipotent to save.
Captivity is captive led;
For Jesus liveth, and was dead.

Who now accuseth them
    For whom their Surety died?
Who now shall those condemn
    Whom God hath justified?
Captivity is captive led;
For Jesus liveth, and was dead.

    Christ hath the ransom paid;
        His glorious work is done:
    On Him our help is laid,
        By Him our victory won.
Captivity is captive led;
For Jesus liveth, and was dead.

    To God, the Risen Son,
        Father and Spirit blest,
   'Eternal Three in One,
        All worship be addrest.
Captivity is captive led;
For Jesus liveth, and was dead.

Angels, roll the Rock away!

By Rev. Thomas Scott, a Presbyterian clergyman, born at Norwich, England, and died at Hupton in 1776. It was altered by Rev. Thomas Gibbons, a Congregational minister in England (1720-1785), and is usually ascribed to him. It has passed through many transformations; the original version containing seven verses, and beginning, "Trembling earth gave awful signs." The following is the form given in Dr. Schaff's "Christ in Song," and pronounced by him at least equal to the original, although so changed as to read like quite another hymn.

NGELS, roll the rock away!
Death, yield up the mighty prey!
See! the Saviour quits the tomb,
Glowing with immortal bloom.
    Hallelujah! Hallelujah!
Christ the Lord is risen to-day.

Shout, ye seraphs! angels, raise
Your eternal song of praise!
Let the earth's remotest bound
Echo to the blissful sound!
    Hallelujah! Hallelujah!
Christ the Lord is risen to-day.

Holy Father, Holy Son,
Holy Spirit, Three in One,
Glory as of old to Thee,
Now and evermore, shall be!
    Hallelujah! Hallelujah!
Christ the Lord is risen to-day.

Again the Lord of Life and Light.

By ANNA LÆTITIA BARBAULD, born in Leicestershire June 20, 1743; died at Newington Green in 1825. She was the daughter of a Dissenting clergyman, Rev. John Aikin; and the wife of another, Rev. Rochemont Barbauld. She wrote verses at an early age, and in 1773 published a volume of poems which attained considerable popularity.

AGAIN the Lord of Life and Light
    Awakes the kindling ray,
Unseals the eyelids of the morn,
    And pours increasing day.

Oh, what a night was that which wrapt
    The heathen world in gloom!
Oh, what a sun which broke this day
    Triumphant from the tomb!

This day be grateful homage paid,
    And loud hosannas sung;
Let gladness dwell in every heart,
    And praise on every tongue.

Ten thousand differing lips shall join
    To hail this welcome morn,
Which scatters blessings from its wings
    To nations yet unborn.

The powers of darkness leagued in vain
  To bind His Soul in death:
He shook their kingdom, when He fell,
  With His expiring breath.

And now His conquering chariot-wheels
  Ascend the lofty skies;
While, broken beneath His powerful cross,
  Death's iron sceptre lies.

Exalted high at God's right hand,
  The Lord of all below,
Through Him is pardoning love dispensed,
  And boundless blessings flow.

And still for erring, guilty man,
  A Brother's pity flows;
And still His bleeding heart is touched
  With memory of our woes.

To Thee, my Saviour and my King,
  Glad homage let me give;
And stand prepared like Thee to die,
  With Thee that I may live!

Who Comes?

By WILLIAM LISLE BOWLES, born at King's Sutton 1762; educated at Winchester and Oxford; died at Salisbury April 7, 1850. He was appointed Vicar of Bremhill in 1804, and held that position for the remainder of his life. He was the author of several prose works, and the complete edition of his poems fills two volumes. He was specially distinguished for his sonnets, which gave inspiration to Coleridge's muse; and one of his biographers, Rev. George Gilfillan, characterizes him as the father of modern poetry.

WHO comes (my soul, no longer doubt)
   Rising from earth's wormy sod,
And, whilst ten thousand angels sing,
   Ascends, ascends to heaven, a God?

Saviour, Lord, I know Thee now!
   Mighty to redeem and save:
Such glory blazes on Thy brow,
   Which lights the darkness of the grave.

Saviour, Lord, the human soul —
   Forgotten every sorrow here —
Shall thus, aspiring to its goal,
   Triumph in its native sphere.

The Setting Orb of Night her Level Ray.

By JAMES GRAHAME, born in Glasgow April 22, 1765; and died near that city Sept. 14, 1811. He was a graduate of the University of Glasgow, and studied law at Edinburgh. He left the legal profession to cultivate his poetic gifts; and in 1809 he gratified a long-cherished desire by taking orders in the Church of England. After brief service as curate at Shipton and at Sedgefield, ill health compelled the abandonment of his sacred duties. He left several poetical works, the best known of which is "The Sabbath," from which the following is taken.

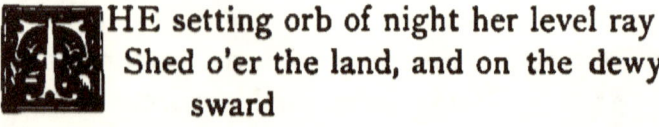

THE setting orb of night her level ray
   Shed o'er the land, and on the dewy
      sward
The lengthened shadows of the triple cross
Were laid far stretched; when in the east
   arose,
Last of the stars, day's harbinger. No sound
Was heard, save of the watching soldier's
   foot.
Within the rock-barred sepulchre the gloom
Of deepest midnight brooded o'er the dead,
The Holy One. But, lo! a radiance faint
Began to dawn around His sacred brow;
The linen vesture seemed a snowy wreath,
Drifted by storms into a mountain cave;
Bright, and more bright, the circling halo
   beamed
Upon that face, clothed in a smile benign,

Though yet exanimate.   Nor long the reign
Of death: the eyes that wept for human griefs
Unclose, and look around with conscious joy.
Yes: with returning life, the first emotion
That glowed in Jesus' breast of love was joy
At man's redemption, now complete; at death
Disarmed; the grave transformed into the couch
Of faith; the resurrection and the life.
Majestical He rose: trembled the earth;
The ponderous gate of stone was rolled away;
The keepers fell; the angel, awe-struck, sunk
Into invisibility; while forth
The Saviour of the world walked, and stood
Before the sepulchre, and viewed the clouds
Impurpled glorious by the rising sun.

He's gone! see where His Body lay.

By Thomas Kelly, born at Dublin in 1769; died May 14, 1855. He was the son of the Right Hon. Chief Baron Kelly, and studied at Dublin University. He abandoned the study of law for theology, and took orders in 1792. Becoming dissatisfied with the Established Church, he left it, and founded a sect which bore his name. He was a man of wealth and learning, and wrote nearly eight hundred hymns, some of which have come into very general use. The following is the original version of a hymn which appears in an abridged and altered form in "Hymns Ancient and Modern," and in many hymnals.

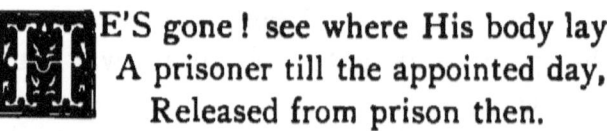E'S gone! see where His body lay,
A prisoner till the appointed day,
    Released from prison then.
Why seek the living with the dead?
Remember what the Saviour said, —
    That He should rise again.

O joyful sound! O glorious hour!
When Jesus, by almighty power,
    Revived, and left the grave.
In all His works behold Him great!
Before, Almighty to create;
    Almighty now to save!

"The first begotten from the dead,"
Behold Him risen, His people's Head,
    To make their life secure:

They too, like Him, shall yield their breath,
Like Him shall burst the bands of death,
   Their resurrection sure.

Why should His people now be sad?
None have such reason to be glad,
   As reconciled to God.
Jesus the mighty Saviour lives:
To them eternal life He gives,
   The purchase of His blood.

Why should His people fear the grave?
Since Jesus will their spirits save,
   And raise their bodies too.
What though this earthly house shall fail?
Almighty power will yet prevail,
   And build it up anew.

Ye ransomed, let your praise resound,
And in your Master's work abound
   With strong and patient faith!
Be sure your labor's not in vain:
Your bodies shall be raised again,
   No more to suffer death.

Come, ye Saints, look here, and wonder.

By Thomas Kelly, 1769-1855. — See note to the preceding hymn.

COME, ye saints, look here, and won-
  der;
  See the place where Jesus lay:
He has burst His bands asunder;
 He has borne our sins away:
  Joyful tidings!
 Yes, the Lord has risen to-day.

Jesus triumphs! Sing ye praises:
 By His death He overcame:
Thus the Lord His glory raises,
 Thus He fills His foes with shame.
  Sing ye praises, —
 Praises to the Victor's name.

Jesus triumphs! Countless legions
 Come from heaven to meet their King:
Soon, in yonder blessed regions,
 They shall join His praise to sing;
  Songs eternal
 Shall through heaven's high arches ring.

Who is this that comes from Edom?

By Thomas Kelly, 1769-1855. — See note to the hymn, "He's gone! see where His body lay."

WHO is this that comes from Edom,
    All His raiment stained with blood,
  To the captive speaking freedom,
    Bringing and bestowing good?
Glorious in the garb He wears,
Glorious in the spoil He bears.   Alleluia!

Tis the Saviour, now victorious,
  Travelling onward in His might;
'Tis the Saviour: oh, how glorious
  To His people is the sight!
Satan conquered, and the grave,
Jesus now is strong to save.   Alleluia!

This the Saviour has effected
  By His mighty arm alone.
See the throne for Him erected!
  'Tis an everlasting throne;
'Tis the great reward He gains,
Glorious fruit of all His pains.   Alleluia!

Mighty Victor, reign forever;
  Wear the crown so dearly won :
Never shall thy people, never,
  Cease to sing what Thou hast done :
Thou hast quelled Thy people's foes,
Thou hast healed Thy people's woes. Alleluia!

The Lord is risen indeed.

By Thomas Kelly, 1769-1855.

THE Lord is risen indeed;
  And are the tidings true?
  Yes, we beheld the Saviour bleed,
  And saw Him living too.

The Lord is risen indeed :
  Then Justice asks no more ;
Mercy and Truth are now agreed,
  Who stood opposed before.

The Lord is risen indeed :
  Then is His task performed ;
The captive surety now is freed,
  And death our foe disarmed.

THE LORD IS RISEN INDEED.

The Lord is risen indeed:
   Then Hell has lost his prey;
With Him is risen the ransomed seed,
   To reign in endless day.

The Lord is risen indeed:
   He lives to die no more;
He lives the sinner's cause to plead,
   Whose curse and shame He bore.

The Lord is risen indeed:
   This yields my soul a plea;
He bore the punishment decreed;
   This satisfies for me.

The Lord is risen indeed:
   Attending angels, hear!
Up to the courts of heaven with speed
   The joyful tidings bear.

Then take your golden lyres,
   And strike each cheerful chord,
Join all the bright celestial choirs,
   To sing our Risen Lord.

Morning of the Sabbath Day.

By James Montgomery, born at Irvine, in Ayrshire, Nov. 4, 1771; died at Sheffield April 30, 1854. He was of Irish parentage, and his father was a Moravian minister. He was himself designed for the ministry; but his tastes led him into literary pursuits, and he became editor of the Sheffield "Iris" in 1795. He was twice imprisoned for reflections upon the government; and it was in prison, in 1797, that he commenced writing verses. His poems won and held a large measure of popularity, and his hymns in particular may be regarded as a permanent legacy to sacred literature. He was of a pure and generous character, and his life was long and tranquil. Among his longer poems are "The Ocean," "The Wanderer," "The West Indies," "The World before the Flood," "Greenland," and "The Pelican Island."

MORNING of the Sabbath day,
   O thou sweetest hour of prime!
Dart a retrospective ray
   O'er the eastern hills of time;
Daybreak let my spirit see
At the foot of Calvary.

Joseph's sepulchre is nigh;
   Here the seal upon the stone;
There the sentinel, with eye
   Star-like fixed on that alone.
All around is calm and clear:
Life and death keep Sabbath here.

Bright and brighter, beam on beam,
  Now, like first created light,
From the rock-cleft, gleam by gleam,
  Shoots athwart the waning night,
Till the splendor grows intense,
Overpowering mortal sense.

Glory turns with me to gloom,
  Sight, pulsation, thought, depart;
And the stone that closed the tomb
  Seems to lie upon my heart.
With that shock the vision flies:
Christ is risen, and I may rise, —

Rise, like Him, as from this trance,
  When the trumpet calls the just
To the saints' inheritance
  From their dwellings in the dust.
By thy resurrection's power,
Jesus, save me in that hour!

Sabbath morning, hail to thee!
  O thou sweetest hour of prime!
From the foot of Calvary
  Now to Zion's top I climb,
There my risen Lord to meet,
In His temple, at His feet.

Lo! the Day the Lord hath made!

By Bishop RICHARD MANT, born at Southampton in 1776; died Nov. 2, 1848. He graduated at Oxford in 1797; was appointed curate in 1802, and vicar in 1810. In 1813 he was appointed domestic chaplain to the Archbishop of Canterbury; and, three years later, he was made Rector of St. Botolph, London. He was made a bishop in 1820, and presided over the sees of Killaloe, of Down and Connor, and of Dromore. He wrote many hymns and translations, and published also several prose works.

LO! the day the Lord hath made!
From the tomb's funereal shade
Now the Sun of goodness brings
Healing on His radiant wings;
And before His bridal light
All the denizens of night,
Fear, and shame, and sorrow, fade:
Bless the day the Lord hath made!

Angels, who the morn outrun
To adore the glorious Sun,
At whose step the firm earth shakes,
From whose eye the lightning breaks;
Ye, whose hand excels in might;
Ye, whose accents breathe delight;
Forms in dazzling white arrayed, —
Bless the day the Lord hath made!

Holy women, whom the dawn
Sees by pious duty drawn
To the Saviour's rock-hewn bed,
Tears and unguents rich to shed,—
Stay your tears, your gifts withhold;
Angel-led, the cave behold
Where the Saviour's corse was laid:
Bless the day the Lord hath made!

Holy men, beloved pair,
Who with rival speed repair
To explore the inmost gloom
Of the yet untrodden tomb,
Mark the clothes that wrapped Him round,
Swathed His limbs, His temples bound,
All in seemliest order laid:
Bless the day the Lord hath made!

First of all the faithful train
To behold thy Lord again,
Stay not, Mary, weeping here:
See, thy Saviour's self is near!
Quick thy mighty Master greet;
Fall in homage at His feet.
All thy griefs are now repaid:
Bless the day the Lord hath made!

Doubtful hearts, whom late He taught,
Musing now in anxious thought,
Cease your doubts, your sorrows cease;
Hear Him speak the words of peace.
Deem your eyes no spirit meet:
Mark His piercèd hands and feet;
Mark His wounded side displayed:
Bless the day the Lord hath made!

Church of God, whom this fair morn
Sees to life and glory born,
Founded on the living Stone,
Which, by Judah's builders thrown,
Thrown with infamy aside,
Now becomes thy Strength and Pride,
Be thy debt of duty paid:
Bless the day the Lord hath made!

Ever as this day shall rise,
Beaming in the vernal skies,
Duly to the Saviour's praise,
Church of God, the anthem raise!
Christ, our Passover, was slain:
Keep the feast, and swell the strain.
Christ is raisèd from the dead:
Bless the day the Lord hath made!

Morning breaks upon the Tomb.

By WILLIAM BENGO COLLYER, D.D., born at Blackheath, Kent, April 14, 1782; died Jan. 9, 1854. He received only an academic education, and began to preach at the age of eighteen. He was pastor of a congregation at Peckham, Surrey, for fifty-three years. He published several volumes of prose, and one book of hymns.

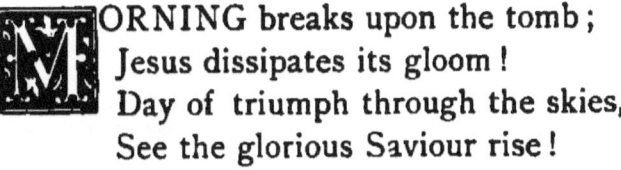ORNING breaks upon the tomb;
Jesus dissipates its gloom!
Day of triumph through the skies,
See the glorious Saviour rise!

Christians, dry your flowing tears;
Chase those unbelieving fears;
Look on His deserted grave;
Doubt no more His power to save.

Ye who are of death afraid,
Triumph in the scattered shade;
Drive your anxious cares away;
See the place where Jesus lay.

So the rising sun appears,
Shedding radiance o'er the spheres;
So returning beams of light
Chase the terrors of the night.

Christ is risen! the Lord is come.

By HENRY HART MILMAN, D.D., who was born in London Feb. 10, 1791; graduated at Oxford 1816; ordained 1817; Vicar of St. Mary's, Reading, 1817-35; professor of poetry at Oxford 1821-31; Rector of St. Margaret's, Westminster, and Canon of Westminster, 1835-49; Dean of St. Paul's 1849; died at Sunningfield, near Ascot, Sept. 24, 1868. He is best known by his great works, the History of the Jews, the History of Christianity, and the History of Latin Christianity, which are characterized by a thorough and fearless scholarship, impartiality of judgment, and eloquence of style. He wrote several biographical and historical essays; edited the writings of several poets; translated from the Sanscrit, Greek, and Latin; and published three volumes of poems, from the second of which the following is taken.

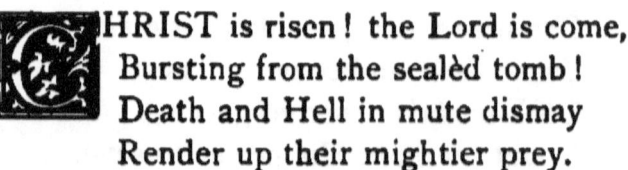HRIST is risen! the Lord is come,
Bursting from the sealèd tomb!
Death and Hell in mute dismay
Render up their mightier prey.

Christ is risen! but not alone!
Death, thy kingdom is o'erthrown!
We shall rise as He hath risen
From the deep sepulchral prison.

Heirs of death, and sons of clay,
Long in death's dark thrall we lay,
And went down in trembling gloom
To the unawakening tomb.

Heirs of life, and sons of God,
On the path our Captain trod,
Now we hope to soar on high
To the everlasting sky.

Mortal once, immortal now,
Our vile bodies off we throw,
Glorious bodies to put on
Round our great Redeemer's throne.

Lofty hopes! and theirs indeed
Who the Christian's life shall lead:
Christ's below in faith and love,
Christ's in endless bliss above.

O Day of Days! shall Hearts set Free.

By REV. JOHN KEBLE, who claims notice as the author of the most popular collection of hymns of the century, and as one of the chief originators of the Tractarian movement in the Church of England. He was born at Fairford, Gloucestershire, April 25, 1792; graduated M.A. at Oxford in 1813; became Curate of Hursley in 1825; but soon after returned to Fairford, where he resided until 1835. About this time he became Vicar of Hursley, and retained that living until his death, March 29, 1866. He was appointed professor of poetry at Oxford in 1831, and wrote early and late, in prose and verse, until the year of his death. His fame rests chiefly upon his "Christian Year," a volume of poems pertaining to the festivals of the Church. This book has had an extraordinary popularity. It was first published in 1827, and the author lived to revise the ninety-sixth edition of it. Dr. Arnold declared that he never saw poems equalling these in the wonderful knowledge of Scripture, the purity of heart, and the richness of poetry, which they exhibit. Keble wrote also the "Lyra Innocentium," a volume of poems on the ways and privileges of children; "The Psalter," a metrical rendering of the Psalms of David; sundry pieces in the "Lyra Apostolica;" and a number of religious, theological, and controversial works in prose.

DAY of days! shall hearts set free
No "minstrel rapture" find for thee?
Thou art the Sun of other days:
They shine by giving back thy rays.

Enthronèd in thy sovereign sphere,
Thou shedd'st thy light on all the year:
Sundays by thee more glorious break,
An Easter Day in every week.

And week-days, following in their train,
The fulness of thy blessing gain;
Till all, both resting and employ,
Be one Lord's day of holy joy.

Then wake, my soul, to high desires,
And earlier light thine altar-fires;
The World some hours is on her way,
Nor thinks on thee, thou blessed day.

Or, if she thinks, it is in scorn:
The Vernal light of Easter morn
To her dark gaze no brighter seems
Than Reason's or the Law's pale beams.

"Where is your Lord?" she scornful asks:
"Where is His hire? we know His tasks:
Sons of a King ye boast to be:
Let us your crowns and treasures see."

We in the words of Truth reply,
(An angel brought them from the sky,)—
"Our crown, our treasure, is not here;
'Tis stored above the highest sphere.

Methinks your wisdom guides amiss,
To seek on earth a Christian's bliss:
We watch not now the lifeless stone;
Our only Lord is risen and gone."

Yet even the lifeless stone is dear,
For thoughts of Him who late lay here;
And the base world, now Christ hath died,
Ennobled is, and glorified.

No more a charnel-house to fence
The relics of lost innocence, —
A vault of ruin and decay:
The imprisoning stone is rolled away.

'Tis now a cell, where angels use
To come and go with heavenly news,
And in the ears of mourners say, —
"Come, see the place where Jesus lay."

'Tis now a fane where Love can find
Christ everywhere embalmed and shrined,
Aye gathering up memorials sweet
Where'er she sets her duteous feet.

Oh, joy to Mary first allowed,
When roused from weeping o'er His shroud
By His own calm, soul-soothing tone,
Breathing her name as still His own!

Joy to the faithful three renewed,
As their glad errand they pursued!
Happy, who so Christ's word convey,
That He may meet them on their way.

So is it still: to holy tears,
In lonely hours, Christ risen appears:
In social hours, who Christ would see,
Must turn all tasks to charity.

Christ hath arisen! O Mountain-Peaks, attest!

By Mrs. FELICIA HEMANS, born at Liverpool Sept. 25, 1793; died at Dublin May 16, 1835. A woman of rare loveliness of character, her life was clouded by domestic trouble, and by long and painful illness; but her verse was always clear, pure, and elevated in sentiment, and exhibited a serene faith. She holds a place among the foremost of the British female poets, and was one of the most prolific writers of her day. The stanzas which follow constitute the concluding portion of her poem, "Easter Day in a Mountain Churchyard."

CHRIST hath arisen! O mountain-peaks, attest!
Witness, resounding glen and torrent-wave!
The immortal courage in the human breast
Sprung from that victory; tell how oft the brave
To camp midst rock and cave,
Nerved by those words, their struggling faith have borne,
Planting the cross on high above the clouds of morn!

The Alps have heard sweet hymnings for to-
  day;
Ay, and wild sounds of sterner, deeper tone
Have thrilled their pines, when those that
  knelt to pray
Rose up to arm! The pure, high snows have
  known
      A coloring not their own,
But from true hearts, which, by that crimson
  stain,
Gave token of a trust that called no suffering
  vain.

Those days are past: the mountains wear no
  more
The solemn splendor of the martyr's blood;
And may that awful record, as of yore,
Never again be known to field or flood!
      E'en though the faithful stood,
A noble army, in the exulting sight
Of earth and heaven, which blessed their
  battle for the right!

But many a martyrdom by hearts unshaken
Is yet borne silently in homes obscure;
And many a bitter cup is meekly taken;
And for the strength whereby the just and pure
      Thus steadfastly endure,

Glory to Him whose victory won that dower, —
Him from whose rising streamed that robe of
     spirit-power!

Glory to Him! Hope to the suffering breast!
Light to the nations! He hath rolled away
The mists, which, gathering into deathlike
     rest,
Between the soul and heaven's calm ether lay.
     His love hath made it day
With those that sat in darkness. Earth and
     sea,
Lift up glad strains for man by truth divine
     made free!

Weeper! to thee how Bright a Morn was given!

By Mrs. HEMANS. — See note to preceding. The following sonnet is upon "Mary Magdalene at the Sepulchre."

WEEPER! to thee how bright a morn
          was given
     After thy long, long vigil of despair,
When that high voice which burial-rocks had
     riven
     Thrilled with immortal tones the silent air!
     Never did clarion's royal blast declare
Such tale of victory to a breathless crowd,

As the deep sweetness of *one* word could
    bear
Into thy heart of hearts, O woman! bowed
By strong affection's anguish! one low word, —
    "*Mary!*" — and all the triumph wrung
        from death
Was thus revealed; and thou, that so hadst
    erred,
So wept, and been forgiven, in trembling faith
Didst cast thee down before the all-conquer-
    ing Son,
Awed by the mighty gift thy tears and love
    had won!

All is o'er; the Pain, the Sorrow.

By JOHN MOULTRIE, who was born Dec. 30, 1799; educated at Eton and Cambridge; ordained deacon in 1825, and priest soon after; and entered the living of Rugby in 1828, which he retained until his death, — from disease contracted at the bedside of a parishioner, — in December, 1874. A complete edition of his poems was published after his death. Moir characterizes him as "a poet of elegant mind, and of considerable pathetic power." Several of his religious poems have come into general use as hymns; and an abridged and somewhat altered version of the following, comprising only the first three and the last verses, is adopted in the Hymnal of the Protestant Episcopal Church, and in several other hymnals.

ALL is o'er; the pain, the sorrow,
    Human taunts, and fiendish spite:
Death shall be despoiled to-morrow
    Of the prey he grasps to-night:

Yet once more, to seal his doom,
Christ must sleep within the tomb.

Close and still the cell that holds Him,
    While in brief repose He lies;
Deep the slumber that infolds Him,
    Veiled a while from mortal eyes, —
Slumber such as needs must be
After hard-won victory.

Fierce and deadly was the anguish
    Which on yonder cross He bore:
How did soul and body languish
    Till the toil of death was o'er!
But that toil, so fierce and dread,
Bruised and crushed the serpent's head.

Whither hath His soul departed?
    Roams it on some blissful shore,
Where the meek and faithful-hearted,
    Vext by this world's hate no more,
Wait until the trump of doom
Call their bodies from the tomb?

Or, on some benignant mission
    To the imprisoned spirits sent,
Hath He to their dark condition
    Gleams of hope and mercy lent? —

Souls not wholly lost of old
When o'er earth the deluge rolled!

Ask no more: the abyss is deeper
   E'en than angels' thoughts may scan.
Come, and watch the Heavenly Sleeper;
   Come, and do what mortals can,—
Reverence meet toward Him to prove,
Faith and trust and humble love.

Far away, amidst the regions
   Of the bright and balmy East,
Guarded by angelic legions
   Till death's slumber shall have ceased,
(How should we its stillness stir?)
Lies the Saviour's sepulchre.

Far away; yet thought would wander
   (Thought by faith's sure guidance led)
Farther yet, to weep and ponder
   Over that sepulchral bed.
Thither let us haste, and flee
On the wings of fantasy.

Haste, from every clime and nation,
   Fervent youth and reverent age,
Peasant, prince,—each rank and station,—
   Haste, and join this pilgrimage.

East and west, and south and north,
Send your saintliest spirits forth.

Mothers, ere the curtain closes
   Round your children's sleep to-night,
Tell them how their Lord reposes,
   Waiting for to-morrow's light;
Teach their dreams to Him to rove, —
Him who loved them, Him they love.

Matron grave, and blooming maiden,
   Hoary sage, and beardless boy,
Hearts with grief and care o'erladen,
   Hearts brimful of hope and joy,
Come, and greet in death's dark hall
Him who felt with, felt for all.

Men of God, devoutly toiling
   This world's fetters to unbind, —
Satan of his prey despoiling
   In the hearts of human kind, —
Let to-night your labors cease;
Give your careworn spirits peace.

Ye who roam our seas and mountains,
   Messengers of love and light;
Ye who guard Truth's sacred fountains,
   Weary day and wakeful night;

Men of labor, men of lore, —
Give your toils and studies o'er.

Dwellers in the woods and valleys;
   Ye of meek and lowly breast;
Ye who, pent in crowded alleys,
   Labor early, late take rest, —
Leave the plough, and leave the loom;
Meet us at our Saviour's tomb.

From your halls of stately beauty,
   Sculptured roof and marble floor,
In this work of Christian duty
   Haste, ye rich, and join, ye poor:
Mean and noble, bond and free,
Meet in frank equality.

Lo, His grave! — the gray rock closes
   O'er that virgin burial-ground:
Near it breathe the garden-roses;
   Trees funereal droop around,
In whose boughs the small birds rest,
And the stock-dove builds her nest.

And the morn with floods of splendor
   Fills the spicy midnight air;
Tranquil sounds, and voices tender,
   Speak of light and gladness there:

Ne'er was living thing, I wot,
Which our Lord regarded not.

Bird, and beast, and insect rover,
　　E'en the lilies of the field,
Till His gentle life was over,
　　Heavenly thought to Him could yield:
All that is, to Him did prove
Food for wisdom, food for love.

But the hearts that bowed before Him
　　Most of all to Him were dear:
Let such hearts to-night watch o'er Him
　　Till the dayspring shall appear;
Then a brighter sun shall rise
Than e'er kindled up the skies.

All night long, with plaintive voicing,
　　Chant His requiem soft and low;
Loftier strains of loud rejoicing
　　From to-morrow's harps shall flow:—
" Death and hell at length are slain;
Christ hath triumphed, Christ doth reign."

'Twas Night! Still Night!

By JOHN HENRY NEWMAN, D.D., born in London in 1801; graduated at Oxford in 1820; tutor of his college for several years; incumbent of St. Mary's, Oxford, in 1828. He shared with Dr. Pusey the leadership of the High-Church party, and established a monastic community at Littlemore in 1842. He was the author of some of the most vigorous of the "Tracts for the Times," and exerted a powerful influence over the young men at Oxford. In October, 1845, he left the Established Church for the Roman-Catholic communion. From 1854 to 1858 he was Rector of the Roman-Catholic University in Dublin. He has written considerable prose on ecclesiastical and controversial subjects, and one or two volumes of verse.

'TWAS night! still night!
 A solemn silence hung upon the scene;
The keen bright stars shone with unclouded light,
 Calm and serene.

 Hushed was the Tomb;
The heavy stone before its entrance lay:
No light broke in upon its silent gloom,
 No starry ray.

 The moonlight beamed;
It hung above that garden soft and clear:
Around the watchful guard its radiance gleamed
 From helm and spear.

The Tomb was sealed:
The watch patrolled before its entrance lone;
The bright night every passing step revealed;
    None neared the stone.

Midnight had passed;
The stars their lustrous shining had decreased,
And daybreak's earliest light was hastening fast
    In the pale east.

The morning star,
Last in the silent Heaven, withdrew its ray;
And the white dawn, spreading its spectre light,
    Foretold the day.

An earthquake's shock
Just at the break of morning shook the ground,
And echoed from that rent and trembling rock
    With startling sound.

The guards, amazed,
Fell to the earth in wonder and affright;
And round the astonished spot in glory blazed
    A sudden Light.

  An Angel there
Descended from the tranquil sky:
The glory of his presence filled the air
  All-radiantly.

  He rolled away
From the still Sepulchre the massy stone;
And, watching silent till the risen day,
  He sat thereon.

  His garments white
Shone like the snow in its unsullied sheen;
His face was like the lightning's gleaming
   light,
  Dazzlingly seen.

  All, all around
Was silence and suspense and listening dread:
The stirless watch lay prostrate on the ground,
  Hushed as the dead.

  At break of day
The Saviour burst that Cavern's stillness
   deep,
Rising in conquest from Death's shattered
   sway
  As from a sleep.

He rose in Power,
In all the Strength of Godhead shining bright,
Fresh as that hallowed Morning's dewy hour,
    Pure as its light.

He rose as God,
Rose as a mighty Victor strong to save,
Breaking Death's silent chain and unseen rod
    There in the Grave.

He rose on high,
While Angels hung around on soaring wing,
Wresting from the dark Grave its victory,
    From Death its sting.

Hail, Day of Joyous Rest!

By HENRY TREND, D.D., born at Devonport Sept. 17, 1804; educated at Bristol and at the University of Giessen; for many years principal of a grammar-school at Bridgewater; Curate of Cannington, and subsequently Minister of the Donative of Durleigh. The latter appointment he held as late as 1869. He is the author of some rather free but very happy translations of old Latin hymns, and of some original hymns, contributed to Mr. Shipley's " Lyræ," the " People's Hymnal," &c. The following is from the " Lyra Messianica."

HAIL, day of joyous rest,
    On which our Lord arose!
Now every Christian breath
    With sacred pleasure glows;

And every Christian tongue should sing
An Easter-song to Sion's King.

 Ah! erst, on midnight ground,
 In sorrow He was found
 Bedewed with His own Blood,
 While crying unto God:
Strange was that bitter agony
He felt in thee, Gethsemane!

 And on the mystic Cross
 He suffered wondrous loss;
 Midst pain and foul disgrace
 His Father hid His face;
And earth and hell were active then
To crush the Friend of friendless men.

 He died; and Joseph's tomb
 Gave the predicted room
 To bury Him; and there
 With stern and jealous care,
To make it sure, they sealed the stone,
And left Him with their guards alone.

 But all their craft and power
 Availed them not that hour:
 The appointed time was come,
 And forthwith from the tomb

He rose; for, lo! the astonished rock
Was shivered as by earthquake-shock.

Yes, Jesus left the grave,
  And took His life again;
And now He lives to save
  The dying sons of men:
Let His triumphant praise be sung
Through every land, by every tongue.

Arise, my Soul, arise!

By Mrs. SARAH FLOWER ADAMS, who was born in Cambridge Feb. 22, 1805; and died Aug. 13, 1849. She was the daughter of an editor, and the wife of William Bridges Adams, an eminent engineer, and contributor to journals and reviews. She contributed prose and poetry to the periodicals, and published a dramatic poem, but is most widely known by her hymns, and particularly by that one beginning, "Nearer, my God, to Thee," which has become the property of the Church universal.

ARISE,
    My soul, arise!
  Sing, with thy latest breath,
Christ's conquest over death.
    Arise,
    My soul, arise!
Sing it unto the skies;
Sing it over the earth, and under;

There, 'mongst the myriad graves
    Of kings or slaves,
Let the song pierce their urns asunder.
      Arise,
         Our souls, arise!
In heaven the angel-band
Stand ready, — in each hand
  A palm to wave;
On earth a listening throng
Wait the redeeming song,
  Their souls to save;
Below, all silently,
The dead attend the cry:
        O grave!
Where is thy victory?
  The branches wave;
Our Lord hath risen on high!
        O death!
Where is thy sting?
  The dust beneath
Stirs while we sing.
O grave! where is thy victory?
O death! where is thy sting!
      Arise,
         Our souls, arise!

To Him who for our Sins was slain.

By ARTHUR TOZER RUSSELL, born at Northampton March 20, 1806; graduated at Cambridge; ordained priest in 1830; appointed Vicar of Caxton in the same year; and afterward incumbent of the vicarages of Whaddon, of Toxteth Park, near Liverpool, and of Wellington, Salop. He has written and edited several volumes of hymns, and has also published several books of sermons and essays.

TO Him who for our sins was slain,
To Him, for all His dying pain,
  Sing we Alleluia!

To Him the Lamb our Sacrifice,
Who gave His blood our ransom-price,
  Sing we Alleluia!

To Him who died that we might die
To sin, and live with Him on high,
  Sing we Alleluia!

To Him who rose that we might rise,
And reign with Him beyond the skies,
  Sing we Alleluia!

To Him who now for us doth plead,
And helpeth us in all our need,
  Sing we Alleluia!

To Him who doth prepare on high
Our home in immortality,
               Sing we Alleluia!

To Him be glory evermore;
Ye heavenly hosts, your Lord adore:
               Sing we Alleluia!

To Father, Son, and Holy Ghost,
Our God most great, our joy, our boast,
               Sing we Alleluia!

In the Tomb, behold, He lies.

By ARTHUR TOZER RUSSELL. — See note to preceding.

IN the tomb, behold, He lies
  Who the dead awaketh:
Christ, our stricken sacrifice,
  Of sweet rest partaketh.

Fear we, then, no more the gloom
  Of Death's narrow dwelling:
Jesus died! the wondering tomb
  Of His praise is telling.

Vainly shall His foes rejoice,
  Vainly Death detain Him:

Lazarus heard His wakening voice:
  What can, then, restrain Him?

What shall bind His conquering arm
  Who the mountains rendeth,
And, that He may Death disarm,
  To the tomb descendeth?

In Thy glorious Resurrection.

By Bishop CHRISTOPHER WORDSWORTH, born in 1807; graduated at Trinity College, Cambridge, with high honors, in 1830; received priest's orders in 1835; head master of Harrow School in 1836; Canon of Westminster Abbey in 1844; Vicar of Stanford-in-the-Vale, Berks, in 1850; Archdeacon of Westminster in 1865; Bishop of Lincoln in 1868. He has written much in prose, and has published a volume of hymns, entitled "Holy Year," from which the following is taken. He is a nephew of William Wordsworth.

IN Thy glorious Resurrection,
  Lord, we see a world's erection;
    Man in Thee is glorified:
Bliss for which the Patriarchs panted,
Joys by ancient sages chanted,
  Now in Thee are verified.

Oracles of former ages,
Veiled in dim prophetic pages,
  Now lie open to the sight;

IN THY GLORIOUS RESURRECTION.

Now the Types, which glimmered darkling
In the twilight gloom, are sparkling
  In the blaze of noonday light.

Isaac from the wood is risen;
Joseph issues from the prison;
  See the Paschal Lamb which saves;
Israel through the sea is landed;
Pharaoh and his hosts are stranded,
  And o'erwhelmèd in the waves.

See the cloudy Pillar leading,
Rock refreshing, Manna feeding;
  Joshua fights, and Moses prays:
See the lifted wave-sheaf, cheering, —
Pledge of Harvest-fruits appearing,
  Joyful dawn of happy days.

Samson see at night uptearing
Gaza's brazen gates, and bearing
  To the top of Hebron's hill;
Jonah comes from stormy surges,
From his three-days' grave emerges,
  Bids beware of coming ill.

Thus Thy Resurrection glory
Sheds a light on ancient story;
  And it casts a forward ray, —

Beacon-light of solemn warning,
To the dawn of that great morning,
   Ushering in the Judgment-Day.

Ever since Thy death and rising,
Thou the nations art baptizing
   In Thy death's similitude:
Dead to sin, and ever dying,
And our members mortifying,
   May we walk with life renewed!

Forth from Thy first Easter going,
Sundays are forever flowing
   Onward to a boundless sea:
Lord, may they for Thee prepare us,
On a holy river bear us
   To a calm eternity!

Glory be to God the Father;
And to Him who all does gather
   In Himself, the Eternal Son,
And the dead to life upraises;
And to Holy Ghost be praises:
   Glory to the Three in One!

The Tomb is Empty: wouldst thou have it Full?

By HORATIUS BONAR, D.D., born at Edinburgh in 1808. He graduated at the University of Edinburgh, and was ordained to the ministry in 1837, and since that time has been pastor at Kelso. He joined the Free Church of Scotland in 1843. He is the author of numerous prose works of a devotional character, and of three series of "Hymns of Faith and Hope."

THE tomb is empty: wouldst thou have it full,
   Still sadly clasping the unbreathing clay?
O weak in faith, O slow of heart, and dull,
To dote on darkness, and shut out the day!

The tomb is empty: He who three short days,
After a sorrowing life's long weariness,
Found refuge in this rocky resting-place,
Has now ascended to the throne of bliss.

Here lay the Holy One, the Christ of God;
He who for death gave death, and life for life;
Our heavenly Kinsman, our true flesh and blood;
Victor for us on hell's dark field of strife.

This was the Bethel, where, on stony bed,
While angels came and went from morn till even,
Our truer Jacob laid his wearied head:
This was to him the very gate of heaven.

The Conqueror, not the conquered, He to whom
The keys of death and of the grave belong,
Crossed the cold threshold of the stranger's tomb,
To spoil the spoiler, and to bind the strong.

Here Death had reigned: into no tomb like this
Had man's fell foe aforetime found his way;
So grand a trophy ne'er before was his,
So vast a treasure, so divine a prey.

But no: his triumph ends; the rock-barred door
Is opened wide, and the Great Prisoner gone:
Look round and see, upon the vacant floor,
The napkin and the grave-clothes lie alone.

Yes: Death's last hope, his strongest fort and prison,
Is shattered, never to be built again;

And He, the mighty Captive, He is risen,
Leaving behind the gate, the bar, the chain.

Yes, He is risen who is the First and Last;
Who was and is; who liveth, and was dead:
Beyond the reach of death He now has passed,
Of the one glorious Church the glorious Head.

The tomb is empty: so, ere long, shall be
The tombs of all who in this Christ repose:
They died with Him who died upon the tree;
They live and rise with Him who lived and
  rose.

Death has not slain them; they are freed, not
  slain;
It is the gate of life, and not of death,
That they have entered; and the grave in
  vain
Has tried to stifle the immortal breath.

All that was death in them is now dissolved;
For death can only what is death's destroy;
And, when this earth's short ages have re-
  volved,
The disimprisoned life comes forth with joy.

Their life-long battle with disease and pain
And mortal weariness is over now:

Youth, health, and comeliness return again;
The tear has left the cheek, the sweat the
    brow.

They are not tasting death, but taking rest
On the same holy couch where Jesus lay,
Soon to awake all glorified and blest,
When day has broke, and shadows fled away.

The Calm of blessed Night.

By HENRY ALFORD, D.D., late Dean of Canterbury, who was born in London in 1810, and died Jan. 12, 1871. He graduated at Trinity College, Cambridge, and won a high reputation as a sound and eloquent preacher, and a biblical critic. He was appointed Dean of Canterbury in 1857. He published several volumes of sermons, a volume of essays on the Greek Poets, and two volumes of poetry. He edited a hymnal called "The Year of Praise," to which he contributed fifty-five hymns. The great work of his life was the Greek Testament, with Notes, and the New Testament for English Readers, — which are among the most valuable products of biblical scholarship.

THE calm of blessed Night
    Is on Judæa's hills;
    The full-orbed moon with cloudless
        light
Is sparkling on their rills:
One spot above the rest
    Is still and tranquil seen, —

The chamber as of something blest
    Amidst its bowers of green.

Around that spot each way
    The figures ye may trace
Of men-at-arms in grim array,
    Girding the solemn place:
But other bands are there;
    And, glistening through the gloom,
Legions of angels, bright and fair,
    Throng to that wondrous tomb.

"Praise be to' God on high!
    The triumph-hour is near;
The Lord hath won the victory;
    The foe is vanquished here!
Dark Grave, yield up the dead!
    Give up thy prey, thou Earth!
In death He bowed His sacred head;
    He springs anew to birth!

Sharp was the wreath of thorns
    Around His suffering brow;
But glory rich His head adorns,
    And Angels crown Him now.
Roll yonder rock away
    That bars the marble gate,
And gather we in bright array
    To swell the Victor's state.

Hail, hail, hail!
 The Lord is risen indeed!
 The curse is made of none avail:
 The sons of men are freed!"

Christ is risen! Alleluia!

By JOHN S. B. MONSELL, born at Derry in 1811. His father was Archdeacon of Derry, and Precentor of Christ-Church Cathedral. The son graduated at Trinity College, Dublin, in 1832; was ordained deacon in 1834, and priest in the year following. He was for a time Rector of Ramoan, and Chancellor of the diocese of Connor; but since 1853 has been Vicar of Egham. He has written much in prose and verse; and his "Hymns of Love and Praise for the Christian Year," from which the following is taken, are deservedly popular.

CHRIST is risen! Alleluia!
 Risen our victorious Head!
 Sing His praises! Alleluia!
 Christ is risen from the dead!
Gratefully our hearts adore Him,
 As His light once more appears,
Bowing down in joy before Him,
 Rising up from grief and tears.
  Christ is risen! Alleluia!
   Risen our victorious Head!
   Sing his praises! Alleluia!
    Christ is risen from the dead!

Christ is risen! all the sadness
   Of our Lenten fast is o'er;
Through the open gates of gladness
   He returns to life once more:
Death and hell before Him bending,
   He doth rise the victor now,
Angels on His steps attending,
   Glory round His wounded brow.
      Christ is risen!   Alleluia!

Christ is risen! all the sorrow
   That last evening round Him lay
Now hath found a glorious morrow
   In the rising of to-day;
And the grave its first-fruits giveth,
   Springing up from holy ground:
He was dead, but now He liveth;
   He was lost, but He is found.
      Christ is risen!   Alleluia!

Christ is risen! henceforth never
   Death or hell shall us inthrall;
Be we Christ's, in Him forever
   We have triumphed over all;
All the doubting and dejection
   Of our trembling hearts have ceased:
'Tis His day of resurrection;
   Let us rise, and keep the feast.

All hail! Dear Conqueror! all hail!

By FREDERICK WILLIAM FABER, D.D., born June 28, 1814; died Sept. 26, 1863. He was the author of some of the most fervent and beautiful hymns in the language. He graduated at Oxford in 1836, and was for several years a college tutor and fellow. He was ordained priest in 1839. In 1843 he became Rector at Elton, in Huntingdonshire; and two years later, after a long mental struggle, he joined the Roman-Catholic Church. In 1849 he established the Brotherhood of the London "Oratorians;" which was removed in 1854 to Brompton, at which place Faber resided until his death. The list of his works includes several books in prose, of a devotional order, sermons, etc., and five volumes of poetry, mostly religious. There is an American edition of his hymns, collected from these volumes.

ALL hail! dear Conqueror! all hail!
   Oh, what a victory is Thine!
How beautiful Thy Strength appears!
   Thy crimson Wounds, how bright
      they shine!

Down, down, all lofty things on earth,
   And worship Him with joyous dread!
O Sin! thou art outdone by love!
   O Death! thou art discomfited!

Ye Heavens, how sang they in your courts,
   How sang the angelic choir that day,
When from His tomb the imprisoned God,
   Like the strong sunrise, broke away?

Oh! I am burning so with love,
  I fear lest I should make too free:
Let me be silent, and adore
  Thy glorified Humanity.

Ah! now Thou sendest me sweet tears:
  Fluttered with love, my spirits fail.
What shall I say? Thou knowest my heart.
  All hail! dear Conqueror! all hail!

Jesus! in Spices wrapped, and laid.

By FREDERICK WILLIAM FABER, D.D. — See note to the preceding hymn. The following is from the poem on "The Life of Our Lord," being a portion of the fifth section, which relates "what was done after His death, burial, resurrection, ascension, session, and second advent."

JESUS! in spices wrapped, and laid
  Within the garden's rocky shade,
    By jealous seals made sure,
Embalm me with Thy grace, and hide
Thy servant in Thy wounded Side,
    A heavenly sepulture!

Jesus! who to the spirits went
And preached the new enfranchisement
    Thy recent death had won,

Absolve me, Lord! and set me free
From self and sin, that I may be
   Bondsman to Thee alone.

Jesus! who from the dead arose,
And straightway sought to comfort those
   Whose weak faith mourned for Thee,
Oh, may I rise from sin and earth,
And so make good that second birth
   Which Thou hast wrought in me!

Jesus! who wert at Emmaus known
In breaking bread, and thus art shown
   Unto Thy people now,
Oh, may my heart within me burn
When at the Altar I discern
   Thy Body, Lord, and bow!

Jesus! amid yon olives hoar,
Thy forty days of sojourn o'er,
   Thou didst ascend on high:
Oh, thither may my heart and mind
Ascend, their home and harbor find,
   With Jesus in the sky!

Sabbath of the Saints of Old.

By Rev. Thomas Whytehead, born at Thormanby, York, in 1815; died in New Zealand in 1842. He graduated at Cambridge, and among his university honors was the chancellor's medal for English verse. He was appointed chaplain to the Bishop of New Zealand, but died soon after reaching his post. The following hymn is abridged and altered by the compilers of "Hymns Ancient and Modern." The complete hymn as given below is contained in Mrs. Alexander's "Sunday Book of Poetry."

SABBATH of the saints of old,
    Day of mysteries manifold,
    By the great Creator blest,
    Type of His eternal rest,
I with thoughts of thee would seek
To sanctify the closing week.

Resting from His work, the Lord
Spake to-day the hallowing word;
And, His wondrous labors done,
Now the everlasting Son
Gave to heaven and earth the sign
Of a wonder more divine.

Resting from His work to-day,
In the tomb the Saviour lay;

His sacred form, from head to feet,
Swathèd in the winding-sheet,
Lying in the rock alone,
Hid beneath the sealèd stone.

All the seventh day long, I ween,
Mournful watched the Magdalene,
Rising early, resting late,
By the sepulchre to wait,
In the holy garden glade,
Where her buried Lord was laid.

So with Thee, till life shall end,
I would solemn vigil spend :
Let me hew Thee, Lord, a shrine
In this rocky heart of mine,
Where, in pure embalmèd cell,
None but Thou mayst ever dwell.

Myrrh and spices I will bring,
My poor affection's offering,
Close the door from sight and sound
Of the busy world around,
And in patient watch remain
Till my Lord appear again.

Then, the new creation done,
Shall be Thy endless rest begun :

Jesu, keep me safe from sin,
That I with them may enter in,
And danger past, and toil at end,
To Thy resting-place ascend.

"What said He, Mary, unto thee?"

By DORA GREENWELL, who was born early in the present century. She is the author of several volumes of verse, among them "Christina and Other Poems," "Stories That Might be True," and "Carmina Crucis," from the last of which the following is taken. She has written also one or two books of essays.

"WHAT said He, Mary, unto thee?
For it was thine His voice to hear,
When thou wert waiting in the gloom
Of twilight dawn, and by the tomb:
He talked with thee when none were near.
Oh, happy thus thy Lord to see!
What said He, Mary, unto thee?"

"Few words He said to me: I hide
Each word He said within my heart.
Fain had I won Him to abide;
Yet soon I knew that I must part
With Him, my Master, Lord, and Guide.
I met His eye; His voice I heard;
I saw His wounded hands and feet:

He called me by my name; no word
Was ever to my soul so sweet;
And by His tomb He bade me stay
Until the breaking of the day!"

"But see, the hills are all aglow!
The sunrise cleaves its path of gold
Through many a darkened valley low,
And fires the mountain summits cold.
What flowers unclose! what herbs of price!
What costly gums for sacrifice
Are dropping now!" — "The hills are high:
I cannot reach them, lest I die;
And by His cross He bade me dwell
Until the evening shadows fell."
"Yet rise; thy Lord hath risen! Behold,
From Hades now He bears away
The gates, and snatches from the hold
Of death and sin a mighty prey:
His soul hath passed afar! to Him
The darkness shines as doth the day.
Why linger 'mid the shadows dim?
Why watch the place where Jesus lay?"

"Beside His tomb, beside His cross,
He bade me rest! Ye speak in vain,
Who have not known my gain nor loss.
The Master's words are kind and plain:

He calls the wounded not to pain,
The weary unto conflict sore;
He bids the wayworn not again
Retrace their fruitless wanderings o'er.
He led me to this place! He knew
My soul upon the burning plain
Where riseth from the earth no dew,
Where falleth from the heavens no rain;
He tracked my steps 'mid forests old
And tangled, where the flowers awake
In torrid midnight gloom, and hold
Death's revel in the jungle-brake;
Yea! He hath known my soul in cold,
The deadly frost that none can bide;
The formless vapors, white and dim,
Became my shroud, and yet from Him
Concealed me not! Whate'er betide,
I clasp the cross! The earth is wide
And drear and old; the heavens are far!
For guide to me He gave no star;
But near His cross He bade me stay
Until the shadows fled away.

"To me He said not, 'Thou shalt rise
With Me, thy risen Lord, this day,
And be with Me in Paradise:'
Beside the cross He bade me stay.
He met me in the garden's gloom;

But to that garden sweet and dim,
Or through its angel-guarded gate,
He sent me not. I wait for Him
Beside His cross, beside His tomb;
I wait for Him, my soul doth wait,
And by the cross I will abide,
And keep the word my Lord hath given.
Except the cross, and Him who died
Upon it, now in earth or heaven
What own I, claim I? Now below
I seek no further; here is woe
Assuaged forever: now above
I look no longer; here is love!"

The Foe behind, the Deep before.

By JOHN MASON NEALE, D.D., born in 1818; graduated at Trinity College, Cambridge, in 1840; died Aug. 8, 1866. He was early elected warden of Sackville College, and retained that position to the date of his death. He was the author of several important historical works; of three or four books of fiction, now forgotten; of some original hymns, of which the following is the most noteworthy; and of some beautiful translations from the mediæval Latin, and the Greek, which are perhaps the richest legacy to the Christian Church that any translator has left. The " Lyra Britannica " contains the following hymn, with six additional stanzas; but, as these are greatly inferior to the portion here given, it has seemed best to present the hymn in its usual form.

HE foe behind, the deep before,
Our hosts have dared and passed
the sea;

And Pharaoh's warriors strew the shore,
And Israel's ransomed tribes are free.
Lift up, lift up your voices now!
The whole wide world rejoices now!
The Lord hath triumphed gloriously!
The Lord shall reign victoriously!
   Happy morrow,
   Turning sorrow
  Into peace and mirth!
   Bondage ending,
   Love descending
O'er the earth!
   Seals assuring,
   Guards securing,
  Watch His earthly prison:
   Seals are shattered,
   Guards are scattered,
  Christ hath risen!

No longer must the mourners weep,
Nor call departed Christians dead;
For death is hallowed into sleep,
And every grave becomes a bed.
   Now once more
   Eden's door
Open stands to mortal eyes;
For Christ hath risen, and men shall rise.

Now at last,
Old things past,
Hope and joy and peace begin;
For Christ hath won, and man shall win.

It is not exile, rest on high;
It is not sadness, peace from strife;
To fall asleep is not to die;
To dwell with Christ is better life.
 Where our banner leads us
  We may safely go;
 Where our Chief precedes us
  We may face the foe.
 His right arm is o'er us;
  He will guide us through.
 Christ hath gone before us:
  Christians, follow you!

See the Land, her Easter keeping.

By CHARLES KINGSLEY, preacher, poet, novelist, and reformer. He was born June 12, 1819, at Holne Vicarage, Devonshire; and died Jan. 23, 1875. He graduated with honor at Cambridge in 1842; was ordained deacon in July of the same year, and was settled at Eversley, in Hampshire; which place continued to be his home for the remainder of his life. A sturdy physical nature, an active mind, a strong and buoyant faith, sympathies warm and deep, and an indomitable and fearless hatred of oppression in every form, made him a power for good wherever his voice was heard, or his writings read. To him, popularity was of less account than principle; and, both in his novels and his poetry, artistic effect was often sacrificed to the vehemence and passion with which he championed the cause of the weak against the strong.

SEE the land, her Easter keeping,
 Rises as her Maker rose;
Seeds so long in darkness sleeping
 Burst at last from winter snows.
Earth with heaven above rejoices;
 Fields and gardens hail the spring;
Shaughs and woodlands ring with voices,
 While the wild birds build and sing.

You, to whom your Maker granted
 Powers to those sweet birds unknown,
Use the craft by God implanted, —
 Use the reason not your own.
Here, while heaven and earth rejoices,
 Each his Easter tribute bring, —
Work of fingers, chant of voices,
 Like the birds who build and sing.

He is risen! He is risen!

By Mrs. CECIL FRANCES ALEXANDER, wife of Rev. William Alexander, now Bishop of Derry. She is the daughter of Major Humphreys of Strabane, Ireland; and was married in 1850. She has published several books of hymns, and one admirable collection called "The Sunday Book of Poetry." The poem entitled "The Burial of Moses" is the most familiar of her pieces. Her husband, also, has written several volumes of prose and poetry.

HE is risen! He is risen!
   Tell it with a joyful voice:
He has burst His three-days' prison:
   Let the whole wide earth rejoice!
Death is vanquished, man is free;
Christ has won the victory!

Tell it to the sinners, weeping
   Over deeds in darkness done,
Weary fast and vigil keeping:
   Brightly breaks their Easter sun.
Christ has borne our sins away;
Christ has conquered hell to-day.

He is risen! He is risen!
   He has oped the eternal gate:
We are loosed from sin's dark prison,
   Risen to a holier state,
Where a brightening Easter beam
On our longing eye shall stream.

Pain and Toil are over now.

By Mrs. CECIL FRANCES ALEXANDER.—See note to the preceding hymn. The following version—abridged, and somewhat altered from the original—is included in the Episcopal Hymnal. The original has six six-line verses, and may be found in Mrs. Alexander's "Verses for Holy Seasons."

PAIN and toil are over now:
    Bring the spice, and bring the myrrh,
Fold the limb, and bind the brow,
    In the rich man's sepulchre.

Sin has bruised the Victor's heel:
    Roll the stone, and guard it well;
Bring the Roman's boasted seal,
    Bring his boldest sentinel.

Yet the morning's purple ray
    Shall present a glorious sight,—
Stone by earthquake rolled away,
    Angel guard all robed in white.

It is the Noon of Night.

By Miss JEAN INGELOW, who was born in Boston, England, in 1830, and is now living in London. Her life was quiet and uneventful until 1863, when she published a volume of poems, which attracted instant attention by the sweetness and beauty of its contents, and won for its author a place among the foremost contemporary singers. Since that time she has published two or three volumes of poetry, several books for children, and two novels. She exhibits in her life the tenderness, gentleness, and charity which find expression in her verse, and is widely and justly beloved. The following verses are a part of a long poem on the Night of Christ's Resurrection, which the author wrote " in humble imitation " of Milton's majestic Hymn on the Nativity.

IT is the noon of night;
   And, the world's Great Light
   Gone out, she widow-like doth carry her:
The moon hath veiled her face,
Nor looks on that dread place
Where He lieth dead in sealèd sepulchre;
And Heaven and Hades, emptied, lend
Their flocking multitudes to watch and wait the end.

   Tier above tier they rise;
   Their wings new line the skies,
And shed out comforting light among the stars:

But they of the other place
The heavenly signs deface;
The gloomy brand of hell their brightness mars:
Yet high they sit, in thronèd state:
It is the hour of darkness to them dedicate.

. . . .

Last, with amazèd cry,
The hosts asunder fly,
Leaving an empty gulf of blackest hue;
Whence straightway shooteth down,
By the Great Father thrown,
A mighty angel, strong and dread to view;
And at his fall the rocks are rent,
The waiting world doth quake with mortal tremblement;

The regions far and near
Quail, with a pause of fear
More terrible than aught since time began;
The winds, that dare not fleet,
Drop at his awful feet,
And in its bed wails the wide oceán;
The flower of dawn forbears to blow,
And the oldest running river cannot skill to flow.

At stand, by that dread place,
He lifts his radiant face,

And looks to heaven with reverent love and fear;
    Then, while the welkin quakes,
    And muttering thunder breaks,
And lightnings shoot, and ominous meteors drear,
And all the daunted earth doth moan,
He from the doors of death rolls back the sealèd stone.

    — In regal quiet deep,
    Lo! One new waked from sleep!
Behold, He standeth in the rock-hewn door!
    Thy children shall not die;
    Peace, peace! thy Lord is by!
He liveth! they shall live forevermore.
Peace! Lo! He lifts a priestly hand,
And blesseth all the sons of men in every land!

    Then, with great dread and wail,
    Fall down, like storms of hail,
The legions of the lost, in fearful wise;
    And they whose blissful race
    Peoples the better place
Lift up their wings to cover their fair eyes,
And through the waxing saffron brede,
Till they are lost in light, recede, and yet recede.

So, while the fields are dim,
And the red sun his rim
First heaves, in token of his reign benign,
All stars the most admired,
Into their blue retired,
Lie hid; the faded moon forgets to shine;
And, hurrying down the sphery way,
Night flies, and sweeps her shadow from the paths of Day.

But look! the Saviour blest,
Calm after solemn rest,
Stands in the garden, 'neath His olive-boughs;
The earliest smile of day
Doth on His vesture play,
And light the majesty of His still brows;
While angels hang, with wings outspread,
Holding the new-won crown above His saintly head.

I have no Wit, no Words, no Tears.

By CHRISTINA GEORGINA ROSSETTI, who was born in London December, 1830, and is now living there. She is the author of several volumes of poems, "Goblin Market," "The Prince's Progress," &c., a book of nursery rhymes entitled "Sing-Song," and a book in prose, "Common-Place and other Short Stories."

I HAVE no wit, no words, no tears;
   My heart within me like a stone
   Is numbed too much for hopes or fears:
Look right, look left, I dwell alone.
I lift my eyes, but, dimmed with grief,
   No everlasting hills I see:
My life is in the falling leaf:
   O Jesus, quicken me!

My life is like a faded leaf,
   My harvest dwindled to a husk:
Truly my life is void and brief,
   And tedious in the barren dusk:
My life is like a frozen thing,
   No bud nor greenness can I see;
Yet rise it shall,—the sap of spring:
   O Jesus, rise in me!

My life is like a broken bowl, —
   A broken bowl, that cannot hold
One drop of water for my soul,
   Or cordial in the searching cold.
Cast in the fire the perished thing;
   Melt and remould it, till it be
A royal cup for Him, my King:
   O Jesus, drink of me!

He comes! He comes!

By GERARD MOULTRIE, in "Lyra Messianica." Mr. Moultrie is the son of another poet, Rev. John Moultrie. He was born about 1830; graduated at Oxford in 1851; was ordained deacon in 1852, and priest in 1858. He taught at Shrewsbury and elsewhere from 1852 to 1864, and in the last-named year became incumbent of Barrow Gurney, Bristol. He was appointed Vicar of South Leigh, near Oxford, in 1868. He is the author of a volume of "Hymns and Lyrics;" and was one of the editors of the "People's Hymnal," to which he contributed thirty-five pieces.

E comes! He comes! the tomb
   Quickens her pregnant womb,
And life and light spring forth in
     mystic birth.
   The garden flowers exhale
   Scents on the morning gale.
Heaven gives her Angel-guard; her incense,
     earth.

The Grave is swallowed up, and Death must die.
Where is thy sting, O Death? where, Grave, thy victory?

    Fling wide, deep Hell, thy door,
    The Lord of Hosts before!
He bears the blossom of the budding wood.
    The lily sprouts to thee
    Her graft upon the tree;
The Cross is quickened from the living Blood.
    Our Aaron bears His staff no longer dry:
    He smites thy sting, O Death! stays, Grave, thy victory!

    He comes! He comes in might!
    Triumphant o'er the night.
In dread dismay exclaim the powers of Hell, —
    "We hailed Him as the dead:
    With Him our sway is fled;
The first-fruits of the sleepers breaks our spell.
    We hold the dead: He raises all; for He
    Has drawn thy sting, O Death! robbed, Grave, thy victory!"

    Lift up your heads, ye Gates!
    The King of Glory waits;

Awaits the emerald rainbow round His
   throne.
   One-half the ring is set
   On earth: the rest is met
In plighted faith where earth and heaven are
   one.
   The Bride may lift the veil, her Lord to
      see:
   Where is thy sting, O Death! O Grave,
      thy victory?

. . . .

   He comes! He comes! once more:
   Roll back the golden door:
The trumpet sounds: once more the Lord is
   come.
   In second Advent-tide
   He comes to claim the Bride,
And bear the Faithful to their Heavenly home.
   There God shall wipe the tear from every
      eye:
   Where is thy sting, O Death? O Grave,
      thy victory?

Dear Saviour of a Dying World.

By Miss ANNA LÆTITIA WARING, a writer who, choosing to be known only by her hymns, has kept her name and the dates of her life out of the biographical dictionaries. She was born at Neath, South Wales. Her volume of "Hymns and Meditations," from which the following is taken, was first published in 1850; and many editions of it have been printed in England and America. Her hymns are deeply imbued with the spirit of Christianity, and are rich in thought and feeling.

DEAR Saviour of a dying world,
    Where grief and change must be,
In the new grave where Thou wast laid
    My heart lies down with Thee;
Oh! not in cold despair of joy,
    Or weariness of pain,
But from a hope that shall not die,
    To rise and live again.

I would arise in all Thy strength,
    My place on earth to fill,
To work out all my time of war
    With love's unflinching will;
Firm against every doubt of Thee,
    For all my future way
To walk in Heaven's eternal light
    Throughout the changing day;

Ah! such a day as Thou shalt own
　　When suns have ceased to shine, —
A day of burdens borne by Thee,
　　And work that all was Thine.
Speed Thy bright rising in my heart,
　　Thy righteous kingdom speed,
Till my whole life in concord say, —
　　"The Lord is risen indeed!"

Oh for an impulse from Thy love
　　With every coming breath,
To sing that sweet, undying song
　　Amid the wrecks of death!
A "hail!" to every mortal pang
　　That bids me take my right
To glory in the blessed life
　　Which Thou hast brought to light!

I long to see the hallowed earth
　　In new creation rise;
To find the germs of Eden, hid
　　Where its fallen beauty lies;
To feel the spring-tide of a soul
　　By one deep love set free,
Made meet to lay aside her dust,
　　And be at home with Thee.

And then there shall be yet an end, —
  An end how full to bless!
How dear to those who watch for Thee
  With human tenderness!
Then shall the saying come to pass
  That makes our home complete;
And, rising from the conquered grave,
  Thy parted ones shall meet.

Yes, they shall meet, and, face to face,
  By heart to heart be known;
Clothed in Thy likeness, Lord of life,
  And perfect in their own.
For this corruptible must rise,
  From its corruption free,
And this frail mortal must put on
  Thine immortality.

Shine, then, Thou Resurrection Light!
  Upon our sorrows shine!
The fulness of Thy joy be ours,
  As all our griefs were Thine.
Now, in this changing, dying life,
  Our faded hopes restore,
Till, in Thy triumph perfected,
  We taste of death no more.

They bound Him well in the Dungeon Cell.

An Easter carol, by Richard Frederic Littledale, D.C.L. — See the biographical notice prefixed to the hymn, "Our Paschal Joy at last is here."

THEY bound him well in the dungeon cell, —
    His father's best-loved son;
And the iron dole into Joseph's soul
    Its bitter way hath won:
But faith and truth have gained him ruth,
    And loosed the tyrant's chain;
And the exile lone to Egypt's throne
    From prison comes to reign.
The Son of the Father, Almighty to save,
Was laid for three days in the heart of the grave;
But the fetters which held Him no longer may bind,
And He reigneth to-day over ransomed mankind.

He laid him down in Gaza town, —
    The forceful Nazarite;
And the heathen guard kept watch and ward
    To slay him at morning light;

But at midnight he rose from the midst of
    his foes,
  No longer would he stay;
And to Hebron's hill, of his own strong will,
  He carried their gates away.
The Nazarene Captive, Whom Hell had insnared,
Around Whom the hosts of the Evil One glared,
Hath gone from among them in conquering state,
And broken in pieces their bars and their gate.

  Oh! now His rolling chariot-wheels
    Lead bound captivity;
  And, where His Presence He reveals,
    His people bow the knee.
  He takes to Him a priestly Bride;
  And He Himself is glorified,
    And clad in white and gold:
  He sitteth on the royal seat,
  And all the nations at His Feet
    Lay tribute manifold.

  The riddle erewhile spoken
    May now be read with ease, —

The slaughtered lion's token,
　　The honey and the bees.
To-day, in full completeness,
　　The mystery stands good;
Since from the Strong comes Sweetness,
　　And from the eater food.

Hearken to Him as He comes in His might,
Monarch of monarchs, victorious in fight.
Speaks He in anger, the sinner to blame?
Speaks He in sorrow, the dastard to shame?
　　With no reproach for blindness
　　　　He meets His own to-day;
　　In perfect loving-kindness
　　　　Thus only will He say:—
"The winter-time away is past; the rain is
　　gone and o'er;
The flowerets bloom again at last; the birds
　　are heard once more;
And in our land we list afresh the cooing of
　　the dove;
The figs and vines are green and lush: oh,
　　come away, My Love!"

As Spring's sweet Breath after long Wintry Snow.

By Right Rev. ROBERT HALL BAYNES, Bishop of Madagascar. He was born at Wellington, Somersetshire, March 10, 1831; received his preliminary education at Bath; graduated at Oxford, B.A., in 1856, and M.A. in 1859; took holy orders, and was appointed Vicar of St. Paul's, Whitechapel, London, in 1858; Vicar of Holy Trinity, Maidstone, 1862; Vicar of St. Michael and All Saints, Coventry, 1866; and Bishop of Madagascar, 1870. He edited the Canterbury Hymnal and "Lyra Anglicana," and has published several volumes of prayers, sermons, and religious poetry. Besides the compilations already mentioned, and others of "English Lyrics," and "Sacred Poetry," he has published a volume of original poems, "Autumn Memories, and other Verses."

AS spring's sweet breath after long
    wintry snow,
  As land to voyager o'er pathless sea,
As daybreak after weary night of woe,
  Is Easter joy to me.

All Lenten shadows over, and the light
  Around us and within so sweet and strong!
Teach us, O risen Master, how aright
  To sing our Easter-song!

We stand to-day beside Thy open tomb;
  We gaze on "linen clothes" with reverent heed,
And hear the angels whispering through the gloom, —
  "Not here, but risen indeed!"

And all the story of Thy love divine
    Throbs through our hearts, longing, O
        Christ! for Thee:
The bitter chalice, with the deadly wine,
    Was drained to set us free.

The grave is dark no more: a stream of light
    Thou, rising, left behind for all Thine own;
Death's chain is broken by Thine arm of might,
    And rolled away the stone.

Now Easter-light flushes the morning sky:
    Thy form we see, all changed, and yet the
        same.
Master, we kneel before Thee: hear our cry,
    And call us each by name.[1]

When evening shadows lengthen all around,
    And we to Emmaus take our weary way,
With us, O risen Saviour, still be found,
    And turn our night to day!

And from Thy radiant throne of light above,
    Oh! send us, till our desert wanderings
        cease,
Thine own best legacy of tender love,
    Thy sweetest gift of peace.

[1] "Jesus saith unto her, Mary." — John xx. 16.

Then at the last, when all shall wake who sleep,
   Made like to Thee in raiment white and fair,
Oh, bid us welcome to Thy home, to keep
   One endless Easter there!

Alleluia! Alleluia!

From the Canterbury Hymnal, edited by Right Rev. ROBERT HALL BAYNES, D.D. — See note to the preceding hymn.

ALLELUIA! Alleluia!
   Hearts to heaven, and voices, raise;
Sing to God a hymn of gladness,
   Sing to God a hymn of praise.
He who on the cross a Victim
   For the world's salvation bled,
Jesus Christ, the King of Glory,
   Now is risen from the dead.

Now the iron bars are broken;
   Christ from death to life is born,
Glorious life, and life immortal,
   On this holy Easter-morn.
Christ hath triumphed, and we conquer
   By His mighty enterprise:

We with Christ to life eternal
  By His resurrection rise.

Christ is risen, — Christ, the first-fruits
  Of the holy harvest-field,
Which will all its full abundance
  At His second coming yield;
Then the golden ears of harvest
  Will their heads before Him wave,
Ripened by His glorious sunshine,
  From the furrows of the grave.

Christ is risen, we are risen:
  Shed upon us heavenly grace,
Rain and dew, and gleams of glory,
  From the brightness of Thy face,
That we, Lord, with hearts in heaven,
  Here on earth may fruitful be,
And by angel-hands be gathered,
  And be ever safe with Thee.

Alleluia! Alleluia!
  Glory be to God on high,
To the Father, and the Saviour,
  Who has gained the victory:
Glory to the Holy Spirit,
  Fount of love and sanctity.
Alleluia! Alleluia!
  To the Triune Majesty!

We were not with the Faithful Few.

From the Canterbury Hymnal.

WE were not with the faithful few
    Who stood Thy bitter cross around,
    Nor heard Thy prayer for those that slew,
Nor felt that earthquake rock the ground;
We saw no spear-wound pierce Thy side:
Yet we believe that Thou hast died.

No angel's message met our ear
    On that first glorious Easter-day, —
"The Lord is risen! He is not here:
    Come, see the place where Jesus lay!"
But we believe that Thou didst quell
The banded powers of Death and Hell.

We saw Thee not return on high;
    And now, our longing sight to bless,
No ray of glory from the sky
    Shines down upon our wilderness:
Yet we believe that Thou art there,
And seek Thee, Lord, in praise and prayer.

Put on thy Beautiful Robes, Bride of Christ.

By William Chatterton Dix; born at Bristol in 1837, and living (in 1872) in Glasgow. He has contributed a number of sacred lyrics to periodicals, and is the author of a small volume of poetry.

PUT on thy beautiful robes, Bride of
    Christ;
    For the King shall embrace thee
        to-day:
Break forth into singing; the morning has
    dawned,
    And the shadows of night are away.

Shake off the dust from thy feet, Bride of
    Christ;
    For the Conqueror, girded with might,
Has vanquished the foe, the dragon cast down,
    And the cohorts of hell put to flight.

Thou art the Bride of His love, His elect:
    Dry thy tears; for thy sorrows are past.
Lone were the hours when thy Lord was
    away;
    But He comes with the morning at last.

The winds bear the noise of His chariot-
    wheels,
  And the thunders of victory roar:
Lift up thy beautiful gates, Bride of Christ;
  For the grave has dominion no more.

Once they arrayed Him with scorning; but
    see!
  His apparel is glorious now:
In His hand are the keys of death and of hell,
  And the diadem gleams on His brow.

Hark! 'tis her voice: Alleluia she sings,
  Alleluia! the captives are free!
Unfolded the gates of Paradise stand,
  And unfolded forever shall be.

Choir answers choir, where the song has no
    end;
  All the saints raise Hosannas on high;
Deep calls unto deep in the ocean of love
  As the Bride lifts her jubilant cry.

Christ is become our Paschal Lamb.

From Chope's Hymnal.

CHRIST is become our Paschal Lamb,
    For us condemned to die:
Those washed in His Atoning Blood
    The Avenger passeth by.

Hail! Sacred Victim, by whose death
    Death hath been overcome;
Who by Thy Burial hast dispersed
    The darkness of the tomb!

He that was dead now lives again;
    The prison-doors are riven:
Triumphant o'er our ghostly foe,
    He opes the gates of Heaven.

Oh, grant us, Lord, with Thee to die,
    With Thee again to rise;
To spurn the things of earth, and seek
    The treasures of the skies!

Far be Sorrow, Tears, and Sighing!

From Dr. Kennedy's "Hymnologia Christiana."

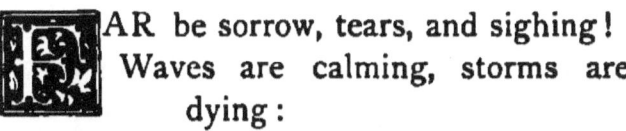AR be sorrow, tears, and sighing!
Waves are calming, storms are dying:
Moses hath o'erpassed the sea;
Israel's captive hosts are free:
Life by death slew death, and saved us;
In His blood the Lamb hath laved us,
Clothing us with victory.   Alleluia!

Hark! the deep abysses thunder;
Hark! the chains are snapped in sunder,
And the unfettered fathers rise,
Soaring toward the opened skies.
God and Man, our ransom paying,
And in light Himself arraying,
Claimeth now the victory.   Alleluia!

Jesus Christ from death has risen:
'Twas His Godhead burst the prison;
'Twas His blest Humanity
Struggled with our misery:

God's long patience, God's rejection,
Brought to pass our resurrection,
　　Brought to pass our victory.　Alleluia!

This the law the Saviour teaches,
This the call the trumpet preaches:—
　　Sinner, from the grave of sin
　　Rise, eternal joy to win.
From the death our sins decreed us
Jesus Christ by death has freed us:
　　Sing we, then, His victory.　Alleluia!

Calm they sit with Closed Door.

From Dr. Kennedy's "Hymnologia Christiana."

CALM they sit with closèd door,
　　Shutting out the city's din:
Tenant of the tomb no more,
　　See the Saviour enter in!
Spirit-like behold Him glide
　To each saintly, wondering guest;
Show His piercèd hands and side,
　Breathe His peace in every breast.

What though years have rolled away,
　Since, triumphant from the tomb,

Jesus, at the close of day,
  Sought that quiet upper room ?
Oft, from Zion's heavenly hill,
  Seeks He yet His faithful few ;
Bides with them in spirit still ;
  Shows each glorious wound anew.

Mighty Lord, descend, we pray,
  Where Thy fond disciples meet :
Many a Magdalene to-day
  Fain would her Deliverer greet ;
Many a Thomas scarce can dare
  Own Thee for his God and Lord :
Come, and banish doubt and care
  With Thy true almighty Word.

Awake, thou wintry Earth!

Contributed by THOMAS BLACKBURN *to Fosbery's "Hymns and Poems for the Sick and Suffering."*

AWAKE, thou wintry earth !
  Fling off thy sadness !
Fair vernal flowers, laugh forth
  Your ancient gladness :
        Christ is risen !

Wave, woods, your blossoms all!
  Grim death is dead;
Ye weeping, funeral trees,
  Lift up your head:
              Christ is risen!

All is fresh and new,
  Full of spring and light:
Wintry heart, why wear'st the hue
  Of sleep and night?
              Christ is risen!

Leave thy cares beneath,
  Leave thy worldly love:
Begin the better life
  With God above:
              Christ is risen!

Glory be to God on High!

By W. B., in "Lyra Messianica."

GLORY be to God on high!
  Sang the Angels from the sky,
  When the Holiest, stooping low,
  Put on strength against our foe.
Ye that hymned the strife begun,
Loftier hymn the triumph won:

Death has crouched to Adam's seed, —
Christ the Lord is risen indeed!

Hail the Flower that ne'er shall fade!
Hail the Day the Lord hath made!
Bridal morn of earth and heaven,
Dawn of joy to Christ's Eleven.
Mary, though the word came true,
Though the sword hath pierced thee through,
Now thy soul no more shall bleed, —
Now thy Son is risen indeed!

Hell hath done its last and worst:
Vain the traitor's kiss accurst,
Swords and staves and ruffian crew,
Priestly vestments rent in two,
Blows, and spitting on that face
Whence the pure heavens look for grace,
Tongues forsworn, and doom decreed, —
Christ the Lord is risen indeed!

Vain the hate that watched His woe,
Feasting on each wound and throe;
From the sacred Corpse drew Blood;
Made Him sure, as best it could:
Hours of grief and waiting past,
Comes our own dear Lord at last,
Ne'er again to groan or bleed, —
Christ the Lord is risen indeed!

Round His feet their snares they laid;
For His Soul a pit they made,
Wrought it deep, and tracked Him well:
Down their own dark gulf they fell;
And their cords, all strong and new,
Lo! like thread He bursts them through!
Hunters caught, and Quarry freed, —
Christ the Lord is risen indeed!

So be all Thy foes undone:
Shine Thy friends like morning sun, —
Shine with light that streams from Thee
In Thy Paschal victory.
While they see Thee standing near,
Darkest times are daylight clear,
Sunlit by the Paschal creed, —
Christ the Lord is risen indeed!

Chants and chimes of Easter-morn,
Praise our God, the Virgin-born,
Who, by dying, death o'erthrew,
Rose, and won us life anew.
Hail! sweet day that stills all fears,
Heals all wounds, and dries all tears;
Mightier yet than bitterest need, —
Christ the Lord is risen indeed!

The Graves grow Thicker, and Life's Ways more Bare.

By. R. E. J. A., in "Lyra Mystica."

THE graves grow thicker, and life's ways more bare,
    As years on years go by:
Nay, thou hast more green gardens in thy care,
    And more stars in thy sky!

Behind, hopes turned to griefs, and joys to memories,
    Are fading out of sight;
Before, pains changed to peace, and dreams to certainties,
    Are glowing in God's Light.

Hither come backslidings, defeats, distresses,
    Vexing this mortal strife;
Thither go progress, victories, successes,
    Crowning immortal Life.

No jubilees, few gladsome, festive hours,
    Form landmarks for my way;
But Heaven and earth, and Saints and friends and flowers,
    Are keeping Easter-Day!

A Pathway opens from the Tomb.

From "Lyra Anglicana," edited by Rev. George T. Rider, New York, 1865.

 PATHWAY opens from the tomb;
   The grave's a grave no more:
   Stoop down; look into that sweet
      room;
Pass through the unsealed door;
Linger a moment by the bed
Where lay but yesterday the Church's Head.

What is there there to make thee fear?
   A folded chamber-vest,
Akin to that which thou shalt wear
   When for thy slumber drest;
Two gentle angels sitting by:
How sweet a room, methinks, wherein to lie!

No gloomy vault, no charnel-cell,
   No emblems of decay;
No solemn sound of passing-bell
   To say, "He's gone away;"
But angel-whispers soft and clear,
And He, the risen Jesus, standing near.

"Why weepest thou? Whom seekest thou?"
   Tis not the gardener's voice,
But His to Whom all knees shall bow,
   In Whom all hearts rejoice, —
The voice of Him Who yesterday
Within that rock was Death's resistless prey.

"Why weepest thou? Whom seekest thou?
   The living with the dead?"
Take young spring flowers, and deck thy
     brow;
   For life with joy is wed.
The grave is now the grave no more:
Why fear to pass that bridal chamber door?

Take flowers, and strew them all around
   The room where Jesus lay:
But softly tread; 'tis hallowed ground;
   And this is Easter-Day.
"The Lord is risen," as He said,
And thou shalt rise with Him, thy risen
     Head.

𝔇𝔞𝔶𝔰 𝔤𝔯𝔬𝔴 𝔏𝔬𝔫𝔤𝔢𝔯, 𝔖𝔲𝔫𝔟𝔢𝔞𝔪𝔰 𝔖𝔱𝔯𝔬𝔫𝔤𝔢𝔯.

Miss CHAPMAN, in her collection of Easter Hymns, credits the following to an English book of Hymns and Carols.

AYS grow longer, sunbeams stronger;
    Easter-tide makes all things new;
Lent is banished, sadness vanished:
    Christ hath risen; rise we too.

Christmas greetings, Twelfth-Night meetings,
    Whitsun sports, are glad and gay;
But the lightest and the brightest
    Of our feasts is Easter-Day.

Earthly story crowns with glory
    Him Whom earthly foes o'ercame:
Victor's laurel ends the quarrel;
    Honor dwells about His name.

Vanquished legions, conquered regions,
    Kings deposed, and princes bound;
Exultation, acclamation,
    Fill His ears, and float around.

Then, unending and transcending
　　Be the glory of the Son;
For transcendent and resplendent
　　Was the victory He hath won.

Death hath yielded, life is shielded,
　　Satan bound, and Hell in chains;
Chased is terror, fled is error;
　　Grief is past, and joy remains.

American.

Welcome, O Day! in dazzling Glory bright!

By WILLIAM ALLEN, D.D., who was born at Pittsfield, Mass., Jan. 2, 1784; graduated at Harvard University 1802; was ordained over the Congregational Church at Pittsfield, October, 1810; President of Dartmouth College 1817; President of Bowdoin College 1820-39; died at Northampton July 16, 1868. He was the author of several biographical and historical works, and of a volume of "Christian Sonnets," from which the following is taken.

WELCOME, O Day! in dazzling glory
    bright!
  Emblem of yet another day most
    blest,
When all Christ's friends with Him in
    Heaven shall rest;
For on this day, in his recovered might,
The Sleeper waked to see this morning's
    light, —
  "The Son of God!" glad angel-hosts attest:
  So, when alive, most fully shown, confest;
For on this day He took His Heavenward
    flight.
When, therefore, our glad eyes this morning's
    sun

See rising on the earth, we'll lift our thought
To Him, who by His death our life hath bought,
And, Victor, King, for us a crown hath won.
It e'er shall be a day of sweetest joy,
Till we shall see our Lord in yonder sky!

Lift your Glad Voices in Triumph on High.

By HENRY WARE, jun., D.D., born at Hingham, Mass., April 21, 1794; died at Framingham Sept. 25, 1843. He graduated at Harvard University in 1812; and, after teaching for some time at the Exeter Academy, he prepared himself for the ministry under the direction of his father, minister of the Unitarian Church at Hingham; was licensed to preach in 1815; and was ordained over the Second Church, Boston, in 1817. He was appointed a professor in the Cambridge Theological School in 1829, and remained in the active duties of that position until the summer of 1842, when, worn out with arduous work as lecturer, preacher, and writer, he retired to Framingham, and died there in the year following. His collected writings were published after his death. They are mostly of a religious and theological character, and include a considerable number of fine hymns, of which the following is the most familiar.

LIFT your glad voices in triumph on high;
For Jesus hath risen, and man cannot die.
Vain were the terrors that gathered around Him,
And short the dominion of death and the grave:

He burst from the fetters of darkness that bound Him,
  Resplendent in glory, to live and to save.
    Loud was the chorus of angels on high, —
    "The Saviour hath risen, and man cannot die."

    Glory to God, in full anthems of joy!
    The being He gave us death cannot destroy!
Sad were the life we must part with to-morrow
  If tears were our birthright, and death were our end;
But Jesus hath cheered the dark valley of sorrow,
  And bade us, immortal, to heaven ascend.
    Lift, then, your glad voices in triumph on high;
    For Jesus hath risen, and man shall not die.

All Praise to Him of Nazareth.

By WILLIAM CULLEN BRYANT, born at Cummington, Mass., Nov. 3, 1794; and died June 12, 1878, at New York. He studied for two years at Williams College, and afterward studied and practised law. In 1825 he became editor of "The New-York Review." In 1826 he formed a connection with "The New-York Evening Post," and, in the year following, assumed the editorial charge of that journal, — a position which he retained until his death, although in later years the direct control of affairs was in other hands. In his long life he found time for many forms of literary activity, and to the last contributed occasional pieces of verse to the periodicals of the day, and graced public occasions by his presence. His noble and elevating poems, and his translations of the "Iliad" and the "Odyssey," give him a permanent place in literature, and justify the estimate in which he is held among English-speaking people. His essays, addresses, and letters of travel, proved him to possess a prose style scarcely less graceful and dignified; and in all his writings, whether in prose or verse, we feel ourselves in contact with a spirit of singular sweetness and purity. The verses which follow were written for a Communion Hymn, and are quoted from a little book of hymns which he published in 1864.

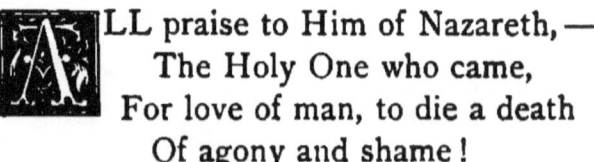

ALL praise to Him of Nazareth, —
    The Holy One who came,
For love of man, to die a death
    Of agony and shame!

Dark was the grave; but, since He lay
    Within its dreary cell,
The beams of heaven's eternal day
    Upon its threshold dwell.

He grasped the iron veil; He drew
  Its gloomy folds aside,
And opened to His followers' view
  The glorious world they hide.

In tender memory of His grave
  The mystic bread we take,
And muse upon the life He gave
  So freely for our sake.

A boundless love He bore mankind:
  Oh, may at least a part
Of that strong love descend, and find
  A place in every heart!

Once more thou comest, O delicious Spring!

By Rev. WILLIAM CROSWELL, D.D., who was born at Hudson, N.Y., in 1804, graduated at Yale in 1823, and died at Boston in 1851. He was Rector of Christ Church, Boston, 1829–40; Rector of St. Peter's Church, Auburn, N.Y., 1840–44; and Rector of the Church of the Advent, Boston, from 1844 till his death. His poems were published in a volume after his death.

ONCE more thou comest, O delicious
  Spring!
And, as thy light and gentle footsteps tread
Among earth's glories, desolate and dead,

Breathest revival over every thing.
Thy genial spirit is abroad to bring
   The cold and faded into life and bloom, —
   Emblem of that which shall unlock the tomb,
And take away the fell destroyer's sting:
Therefore thou hast the warmer welcoming;
For Nature speaks not of herself alone,
But in her resurrection tells our own.
   As from the grave comes forth the buried grain,
So man's frail body, in corruption sown,
   In incorruption shall be raised again.

'Tis He! 'tis He! I know Him now.

By GEORGE WASHINGTON BETHUNE, D.D., who was born in New York in 1805; graduated at Dickinson College 1822; studied theology at Princeton; was settled as pastor over the Reformed Dutch churches at Rhinebeck, N.Y. (1827), at Philadelphia (1834), and at Brooklyn Heights, N.Y. (1850); died at Florence, Italy, whither he had gone to seek recovery of impaired health, April 27, 1862. He was a man of fine scholarship, and of brilliant powers as writer and orator. He published several volumes of essays, sermons, and poems.

'TIS He! 'tis He! I know Him now,
   By the red scars upon His brow,
   His wounded hands, and feet, and side, —
My Lord! my God! the Crucified!

Those hands have rolled the stone away;
Those feet have trod the path to-day;
And round that brow triumphant shine
The rays of Majesty divine.

Oh, from those hands uplifted shed
Thy blessing on my fainting head!
And, as I clasp those feet, impart
The love that gushed from out Thy heart!

Thy death upon the cross be mine;
My life from mortal sin be Thine;
And mine the way Thy feet have trod,
To reign in heaven with Thee, My God!

Tell us, Gard'ner, dost thou know?

By ARTHUR CLEVELAND COXE, D.D., Bishop of Western New York. He was born in Mendham, N.J., May 10, 1818, and studied at the University of New York. He was ordained in 1841, and has been Rector of the parishes of St. Anne's, Morrisania, St. John's, Hartford, and Grace Church, Brooklyn. Since 1864 he has been Bishop of Western New York. He is one of the best known of American sacred poets, and his "Christian Ballads" in particular have enjoyed a wide and merited popularity. The following exquisite Easter Madrigal was first printed in "The New-York Independent" in 1877, and is here given as revised by the author for this collection.

MARY AND SALOME.

ELL us, Gard'ner, dost thou know
Where the Rose and Lily grow, —
Sharon's Crimson Rose, and pale
Judah's Lily of the Vale?
Rude is yet the opening year;
Yet their sweetest breath is here.

GARDENER.

Daughters of Jerusalem,
Yes, 'tis here we planted them.
'Twas a Rose all red with gore;
Wondrous were the thorns it bore
'Twas a body swathed in white;
Ne'er was Lily half so bright.

THE WOMEN.

Gentle Gard'ner, even so:
What we seek thou seem'st to know.
Bearing spices and perfume,
We are come to Joseph's tomb.
Breaks even now the rosy day:
Roll us, then, the stone away.

GARDENER.

Holy women! this the spot.
Seek Him; but it holds Him not.
This the holy mount of myrrh,
Here the hills of incense were,
Here the bed of His repose,
Till, ere dawn of day, He rose.

MAGDALENE.

Yes, my name is Magdalene:
I myself the Lord have seen.
Here I came but now, and wept
Where I deemed my Saviour slept:
But He called my name; and, lo!
Jesus lives, — 'tis even so.

GARDENER.

Yes, the mountains skipped like rams;
Leaped the little hills like lambs;

All was dark, when shook the ground,
Quaked the Roman soldiers round,
Streamed a glorious light, and then
Lived the Crucified again.

WOMEN.

Magdalene hath seen and heard!
Gardener, we believe thy word;
But, oh, where is Jesus fled,
Living, and no longer dead?
Tell us, that we, too, may go
Where the Rose and Lily grow.

MAGDALENE.

Come, the stone is rolled away;
See the place where Jesus lay;
See the lawn that wrapped His brow;
Here the angel sat but now.
"Seek not here the Christ," he said;
"Seek not life among the dead."

ALL.

Seek we, then, the life above;
Seek we Christ, our Light and Love.
Now His words we call to mind:
If we seek Him, we shall find;
If we love Him, we shall know
Where the Rose and Lily grow.

The Winter is over and gone at Last.

By ARTHUR CLEVELAND COXE, D.D., Bishop of Western New York. — See the biographical note prefixed to the preceding poem.

THE winter is over and gone at last;
The days of snow and cold are past;
Over the fields the flowers appear:
It is the Spirit's voice we hear:
    The singing of birds,
    A warbling band,
    And the Spirit's voice,—
The voice of the truth,— is heard in our land.

And gone are the plaintive days of Lent:
The week of the cross with Christ we spent;
Now He giveth us joy for woe:
Gather the flowers, the first that blow:
    The singing of birds,
    A warbling band,
    And flowers, are words
Which even a babe may understand.

And Christ is the song of every thing;
For death is winter, and Christ is spring:

Fountains that warble in purling words,
Hark! how they echo the "song of birds"!
    The singing of birds,
    A warbling band,
    And the purling words
Of brooks and waters, are heard in our land.

Eternal Father! at Whose Word.

By Rev. THOMAS HILL, D.D., born at New Brunswick, N.J., Jan. 7, 1818; graduated at Harvard University in 1843; ordained pastor of the Unitarian church at Waltham in 1845; President of Antioch College, Ohio, in 1859; President of Harvard College 1861-67; representative from Waltham in the Massachusetts Legislature 1870-71; installed pastor of the First Parish, Portland, Me., May 18, 1873. He is the author of a number of theological and scientific treatises, and of several hundred hymns.

ETERNAL Father! at whose word
    Creation flashed to instant birth,
Thy will, which gave this body life,
    Bids it return to lifeless earth.

But thou didst send that risen Lord,
    Who once in Joseph's garden lay,
Burst from the night of transient death,
    And called us to immortal day.

In His dear name we ask thy help,
    By faith in Him to live and die,

That, when our bodies sleep in dust,
  We may with Him ascend on high.

Eternal Father! by thy word
  Raise us from sin and death's dark night,
That we may even now with Christ
  Dwell in the realms of heavenly light.

Sing aloud, Children! sing to the Glorious King.

By Dr. ALEXANDER RAMSAY THOMPSON.—See the biographical notice prefixed to the hymn, "We keep the Festival."

SING aloud, children! sing to the glorious King
  Of Redemption, who sits on the throne;
For the seraphim high veil their faces, and cry,
  And the angels are praising the Son.

With His raiment blood-dyed, and with wounds in His side,
  He returns like a chief from the war,
Where His champion blow hath laid death and hell low,
  And hath driven destruction afar.

Not a helper stood by when the foemen drew
  nigh,
  And arrayed their leagued hosts for the
    fight;
But He met them alone, and the victory won
  By His own irresistible might.

Yes, the triumph He won! Give the Cruci-
  fied Son
  Hallelujahs of praise ever new:
Hail Him, children, and say, Hallelujah! to-
  day;
  For the Saviour is risen for you.

Do Saints keep Holy Day in Heavenly Places?

By Mrs. ADELINE D. T. WHITNEY, who was born in Boston in 1824. She is the daughter of Mr. Enoch Train, and the wife of Mr. Seth D. Whitney of Milton, Mass., where she now resides. She is the author of "Faith Gartney's Girlhood," "Hitherto," "Sights and Insights," and other stories, and of a number of poems, some of which have been published in a volume entitled "Pansies." Her writings, both prose and verse, are marked by deep spiritual feeling.

DO saints keep holy day in heavenly
    places?
  Does the old joy shine new in angel-
    faces?
Are hymns still sung the night when Christ
    was born?
And anthems on the resurrection-morn?

Because our little year of earth is run,
Do they keep record there beyond the sun,
And, in their homes of light so far away,
Mark with us the sweet coming of this day?

What is their Easter? for they have no
  graves;
No shadow there the holy sunrise craves, —
Deep in the heart of noontide marvellous,
Whose breaking glory reaches down to us.

How did the Lord keep Easter? With His
  own!
Back to meet Mary, where she grieved alone,
With face and mien all tenderly the same,
Unto the very sepulchre He came.

Ah the dear message that He gave her
  then! —
Said for the sake of all bruised hearts of
  men, —
"Go tell those friends that have believed on
  me,
I go before them into Galilee.

"Into the life so poor and hard and plain,
That for a while they must take up again,

My presence passes: where their feet toil
    slow,
Mine, shining, swift with love, still foremost
    go!

"Say, Mary, I will meet them by the way,
To walk a little with them; where they stay,
To bring my peace. Watch; for ye do not
    know
The day, the hour, when I may find you so!"

And I do think, as He came back to her,
The many mansions may be all astir
With tender steps, that hasten in the way,
Seeking their own upon this Easter-Day.

Parting the veil that hideth them about,
I think they do come, softly, wistful, out
From homes of heaven that only *seem* so far,
And walk in gardens where the new tombs
    are.

Hallowed forever be that Twilight Hour.

By Mrs. MARTHA PERRY LOWE, born at Keene, N.H., Nov. 21, 1829; and married, Sept. 16, 1857, to Rev. Charles Lowe, editor of "The Unitarian Review." She is the author of two volumes of verse.

HALLOWED forever, be that twilight hour
    When those disciples went upon their way:
The deepening shadows o'er their spirits lower,
    The tender griefs that come with close of day.

A gentle stranger tarried by their side,
    And asked them sweetly why they were so sad?
"Hast thou not seen our Master crucified?"
    They answered. "How can we again be glad?"

"O children," said the stranger, "do you read
    The things which all the holy prophets said,
How He would suffer and would die indeed,
    But yet should rise in glory from the dead?"

And, when the little village came in view,
  They said, "Abide with us; for it is late:"
So He went in, and sat down with the two,
  And took the bread, and blessed it ere they
    ate.

Their searching eyes were fastened on His
    face;
  They caught the look which chained them
    as of old,
Only it wore diviner, loftier grace:
  Their glorious risen Master they behold!

And then they knew how strangely all the
    while
  Their spirits burned within them as He
    talked,
Or listened to them with that very smile,
  Explaining oft the Scriptures while they
    walked.

They felt reward for all their bitter pain,
  When, lo, He vanished softly from their
    sight!
But they could never be so sad again
  Who had the memory of that blessed night.

How shall We keep this Holy Day of Gladness?

By Miss EMILY SEAVER, who was born in Charlestown, Mass., in 1835; and is now living at Rutland, Vt. The following is taken from a volume of poems published in 1878, and containing several excellent hymns for the festivals of the Church.

HOW shall we keep this holy day of gladness,
    This queen of days, that bitter, hopeless sadness
      Forever drives away?
The night is past, its sleep and its forgetting:
Our risen sun, no more forever setting,
      Pours everlasting day.

Let us not bring upon this joyful morning
Dead myrrh and spices for our Lord's adorning,
      Nor any lifeless thing:
Our gifts shall be the fragrance and the splendor
Of living flowers, in breathing beauty tender,
      The glory of our spring.

And, with the myrrh, oh! put away the leaven
Of malice, hatred, injuries unforgiven,

And cold and lifeless form;
Still, with the lilies, deeds of mercy bringing,
And fervent prayers, and praises upward
    springing,
And hopes pure, bright, and warm.

So shall this Easter shed a fragrant beauty
O'er many a day of dull and cheerless duty,
    And light thy wintry way;
Till rest is won, and Patience, smiling faintly,
Upon thy breast shall lay her lilies saintly,
    To hail heaven's Easter-day.

Christ has arisen.

By E. A. WASHBURN, D.D. From Miss Chapman's "Easter Hymns."—See the biographical note prefixed to the hymn, "Still thy sorrow, Magdalena."

CHRIST has arisen:
    Death is no more!
    Lo! the white-robed ones
    Sit by the door.
Dawn, golden morning!
    Scatter the night!
Haste, ye disciples glad,
    First with the light!

Break forth in singing,
  O world new-born!
Chant the great Easter-tide,
  Christ's holy morn!
Chant Him, young sunbeams
  Dancing in mirth!
Chant, all ye winds of God
  Coursing the earth!

Chant Him, ye laughing flowers
  Fresh from the sod!
Chant Him, wild, leaping streams,
  Praising your God!
Break from thy winter,
  Sad heart, and sing!
Bud with thy blossoms fair;
  Christ is thy spring.

Come where the Lord hath lain:
  Past is the gloom:
See the full eye of day
  Smile through the tomb!
Hark! angel-voices
  Fall from the skies:
Christ hath arisen!
  Glad heart, arise!

O mine Eyes, be not so Tearful!

By Miss PHŒBE CARY, who was born Sept. 4, 1824; and died at Newport, R.I., July 31, 1871. Her birthplace was in Ohio, in a farmhouse eight miles north of Cincinnati. Left motherless at an early age, she and her sister Alice found consolation in writing verses, which gradually attracted attention by their grace, compass, and sweetness. In 1850, after publishing a little volume of poems of joint authorship, the sisters went to New York, and began the struggle for a livelihood by literary labor. Six years later they established themselves in a pleasant home on Twentieth Street, which continued the centre of a charming literary and social circle until it was broken by the death of Alice in 1870, and destroyed by the death of Phœbe in 1871. In the annals of authorship there are few things more touching and interesting than the story of the common life, labors, and sorrows of these sister poets, as told by Mrs. Clemmer in her volume of "Memorials." Their lives were as full of fragrance and beauty as their poems, and the latter take rank among the best productions of American female poets. The following poem derives a pathetic interest from the fact that it is the last that Phœbe Cary wrote, and gives voice to her own serene faith, which rose triumphant above pain and sickness and the fear of death.

"MINE eyes, be not so tearful!
Drooping spirit, rise, be cheerful;
Heavy soul, why art thou fearful?

"Nature's sepulchre is breaking,
And the earth, her gloom forsaking,
Into life and light is waking.

. . . .

"Oh the weakness and the madness
Of a heart that holdeth sadness
When all else is light and gladness!

"Though thy treasure death has taken,
They that sleep are not forsaken:
They shall hear the trump, and waken.

"Shall not He, who life supplieth
To the dead seed where it lieth,
Quicken also man, who dieth?

"Yea, the power of death was ended
When He, who to hell descended,
Rose, and up to heaven ascended.

"Rise, my soul, then, from dejection:
See in nature the reflection
Of the dear Lord's resurrection.

"Let this promise leave thee never:—
*If the might of death I sever,
Ye shall also live forever!*"

On Earth was Darkness spread.

Of anonymous authorship; from "A Book of Hymns for Public and Private Devotion," edited by S. Longfellow and S. Johnson.

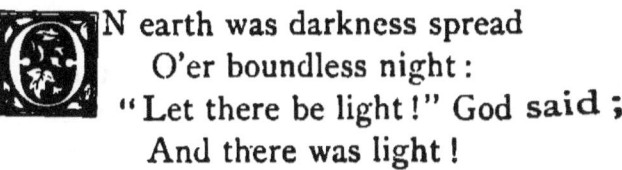

ON earth was darkness spread
   O'er boundless night:
"Let there be light!" God said;
   And there was light!

There hung a deeper gloom
    O'er quick and dead ;
But Jesus burst the tomb,
    And darkness fled.

God by His word arrayed
    Darkness with light ;
God by His Son displayed
    Day without night.

For thee, O man ! arose
    Creation's ray ;
For thee, too, brighter glows
    Salvation's day.

The beams first poured on earth
    For mortals shone ;
The light of later birth
    Immortals own.

Thou that on the First of Easters.

By W. B., from "Elim, or Hymns of Holy Refreshment," edited by Rev. F. D. Huntington, D.D.

THOU that on the first of Easters
    Cam'st resplendent from the tomb,
Leaving all Thy linen cerements
    Folded in the cavern's gloom,

Come with thine "All hail!" to greet us;
　　Come, our Paschal joy to be:
Let our altar, clad in brightness,
　　Yield a throne of white for Thee.

This shall crown the Queen of Sundays;
　　Grant but this, — our cup runs o'er:
Hymns that welcomed in Thine Easter
　　Made us long for this the more.
All the Paschal Alleluias
　　Craved to see the Lamb appear:
Come the hour when faith shall tell us,
　　He is risen! He is here!

Agnus Dei, we are guilty;
　　Panis Vitæ, we are faint;
But Thou didst not rise at Easter
　　To be deaf to our complaint:
Come, oh, come! to cleanse and feed us,
　　Breathing peace, and kindling love,
Till Thy Paschal blessings bear us
　　To the Feast of feasts above.

For Easter Day, O Lilies White!

By HARRIET McEWEN KIMBALL. Miss Kimball was born at Portsmouth, N.H., and has always lived there. She has published a volume of "Hymns," and a volume entitled "Swallow Flights of Song," from the latter of which the following is taken. Mr. Whittier has said of her poems, that, "in the range of modern religious poetry, I know of but few pieces more true and tender, more sweetly touched with the 'beauty of holiness,' than hers."

FOR Easter Day, O Lilies white,
    Your shrinèd splendors keep!
But while the sweet, sad, waning light
    Of Easter Even fades,
    Amid the sacred shades
  Where Sorrow comes to weep, —
Nor weeps in vain,
Since Hope is born of very Pain,
(And Pain its pangs in joy forgets,) —
There breathe your balm, sweet Violets!
Dear twilight-flowers whose lovely hue,
More tender than the tenderest blue,
Yet not as purple sad, appears
Most like transformèd tears.

"A little while!" ye seem to sigh,
  "And yet a little while!" ye say,
  "The stone shall noiseless roll away:
Unseen across the midnight sky

Twilight and Daybreak run to meet!
Already angels throng the air,
And twain, descending, kneel,
  Veilèd in awe, at head and feet
Of that new tomb whose broken seal
The wondering Morning shall reveal,
  And 'He is risen!' declare.
  Sweet odors — sweeter than the sweet
Of violets and lilies blent,
The sweet of holy slumber spent —
  Stealing from vesture folded fair,
  And fragrant with the Lord's own care,
Wherein His Blessed Body lay
Till break of day,
  Shall make most sweet the graves of those,
Who, entering into Paradise,
  Do sleep in Him Who died and rose;
In Whom they, too, shall rise."

Dawn of Dawns, the Easter Day.

By HARRIET McEWEN KIMBALL. — See note to preceding hymn.

DAWN of dawns, the Easter Day
    Far and wide in splendor breaks:
Darkest shadows flee away
        Where it breaks.

Veilèd in its vernal light,
  Christ, the Light of Light, arose;
From the grave's unbroken night
    He arose.

Though beneath the Cross He fell,
  Though upon the Cross He died,
Led He captive Death and Hell
    When He died.

Overcome, He overcame;
  Conquered, more than Conqueror lives;
Crownèd King with Heaven's acclaim,
    Jesus lives!

Through the gates of sacrifice
  He, the Victim, Victor went:
Lo, His triumph lights the skies
    Since He went!

Darker than the night our sin,
  Silent as the tomb our life:
Still His glory enters in, —
    Light and life.

"Rise and follow Me," He saith;
  "Love as I have lovèd you;
Rise to life that I through death
    Won for you."

Love that counts not sacrifice,
  Keeping nothing back from Him, —
To such love must we arise,
    Following Him.

As He laid His garments by,
  With the bondage of the grave
Clothed in Love's own majesty
    Left the grave, —

Self, the earth's most earthy dress,
  Must we cast aside like Him,
And, putting on His righteousness,
    Rise with Him.

He hath rolled the stone away,
  Through Redemption's might, for us:
Dawn of dawns, the Easter Day
    Breaks for us.

Who deems the Saviour Dead?

By Francis De Haes Janvier, who was born in Philadelphia in 1817, and is now residing there. His first volume, "The Skeleton Monk and Other Poems," was published in 1861. In 1863 he published a poem entitled "The Sleeping Sentinel;" and in 1866 a volume of "Patriotic Poems," containing verses written during the war of the Rebellion.

WHO deems the Saviour dead?
   And yet he bowed His head,
   And while in sudden night the sun retired,
   And, through thick darkness hurled,
   Reeled on the shuddering world,
The mighty Son of God in blood expired.

   Expired; but, in the gloom
   And silence of the tomb,
Death's mystery unveiled to mortal sight:
   Triumphant o'er His foes,
   A conqueror He rose,
And from the grave commanded life and light!

   And shall we count those dead
   For whom the Saviour bled,
And died and rose, and lives forevermore?

And were the grief and loss,
The shame and scourge and cross,
Endured in vain by Him whom we adore?

And shall His children fear
When that dread hour draws near
Which gives them immortality with God?
Should not our souls rejoice
To hear our Father's voice,
And gladly take the path the Saviour trod?

Through death's deep shadow lies
Our journey to the skies,
And all beyond is light and life and love:
The dead whom we deplore
Have only passed before,
And wait to greet us in the world above.

Then let the summons come
Which calls our spirits home
From sin and pain and sorrow ever free,
Where weary ones may rest
Upon that Saviour's breast
Whose death revealed our immortality.

The World itself keeps Easter Day.

The following appears in Miss Chapman's volume of Easter Hymns. The name of the author is not given.

THE world itself keeps Easter Day,
    And Easter larks are singing,
    And Easter flowers are blooming gay,
    And Easter buds are springing.
The Lord of all things lives anew,
And all His works are rising too.
    Alleluia! Alleluia! Alleluia!
      Praise the Lord!

There stood three Marys by the tomb
  On Easter morning early,
When day had scarcely chased the gloom,
  And dew was white and pearly:
With loving but with erring mind
They came the Prince of Life to find.
    Alleluia! Alleluia! Alleluia!
      Praise the Lord!

But earlier still the angel sped,
  His words of comfort giving;

"And why," he said, "among the dead
   Thus seek ye for the living?"
The risen Jesus lives again,
To save the souls of sinful men.
   Alleluia! Alleluia! Alleluia!
      Praise the Lord!

The world itself keeps Easter Day,
   And Easter larks are singing,
And Easter flowers are blooming gay,
   And Easter buds are springing.
The Lord is risen, as all things tell:
Good Christians, see ye rise as well.
   Alleluia! Alleluia! Alleluia!
      Praise the Lord!

Breezes of Spring, all Earth to Life awaking.

Anonymous; from "The Changed Cross" collection.

BREEZES of spring, all earth to life
      awaking,
   Birds swiftly soaring through the
      sunny sky,
The butterfly its lonely prison breaking,
   The seed up-springing which had seemed
      to die, —

Types such as these a word of hope have spoken,
  Have shed a gleam of light around the tomb;
But weary hearts longed for a surer token,
  A clearer way to dissipate its gloom.

And this was granted! See the Lord ascending,
  On crimson clouds of evening calmly borne,
With hands outstretched, and looks of love still bending
  On His bereaved ones, who no longer mourn!

"I am the resurrection," hear Him saying!
  "I am the life: he who believes in me
Shall never die: the souls my call obeying,
  Soon where I am forevermore shall be."

Sing hallelujah! light from heaven appearing,
  The mystery of life and death is plain:
Now to the grave we can descend unfearing,
  In sure and certain hope to rise again!

BIBLIOGRAPHY.

The following is a partial list of the volumes consulted in the preparation of this collection:—

LYRA CONSOLATIONIS; or, Hymns for the Day of Sorrow and Weariness. Edited by Horatius Bonar, D.D. New York: 1866.

ELIM; OR, HYMNS OF HOLY REFRESHMENT. Edited by Rev. F. D. Huntington, D.D. Boston: 1865.

CHRISTIAN SINGERS OF GERMANY. By Catherine Winkworth. London: 1869.

THE VOICE OF CHRISTIAN LIFE IN SONG; or, Hymns and Hymn-Writers of Many Lands and Ages. By Mrs. Elizabeth Charles, author of "The Chronicles of the Schönberg-Cotta Family." New York: 1866.

EVENINGS WITH THE SACRED POETS: a Series of Quiet Talks about the Singers and their Songs. By Frederick Saunders. New York: 1869.

ENGLAND'S ANTIPHON. By George MacDonald, LL.D. London.

A BOOK OF HYMNS FOR PUBLIC AND PRIVATE DEVOTION. Edited by S. Longfellow and S. Johnson. 13th edition. Boston: 1861.

LAUDA SYON. Ancient Latin Hymns of the English and Other Churches. Translated into corresponding metres by John David Chambers. London: 1866.

Hymns of Love and Praise for the Christian Year. By John S. B. Monsell, Vicar of Egham. London: 1866.

Hymnologia Christiana; or, Psalms and Hymns selected and arranged in the order of the Christian Seasons. By Benjamin Hall Kennedy, D.D. London: 1863.

Lyra Germanica. Hymns for the Sundays and Chief Festivals of the Christian Year. Translated from the German by Catherine Winkworth. Boston: 1868.

Lyra Messianica. Hymns and Verses on the Life of Christ, Ancient and Modern, with other poems. Edited by Rev. Orby Shipley. London: 1869.

Carmina Crucis. By Dora Greenwell. Boston: 1869.

Sursum Corda: Hymns for the Sick and Suffering. Compiled by the editor of "Quiet Hours," &c. Boston: 1877.

Singers and Songs of the Liberal Faith. Edited, with biographical sketches and historical and illustrative notes, by Alfred P. Putnam. Boston: 1875.

Hymns from the Land of Luther. Edinburgh: 1863.

The Hymns of Denmark. Translated by Gilbert Tait. London: 1868.

Singers and Songs of the Church; being Biographical Sketches of the Hymn-Writers in all the principal collections, with notes on their psalms and hymns. By Josiah Miller, M.A. London: 1869.

Lyra Sacra Americana; or, Gems from American Sacred Poetry. Selected and arranged, with notes and biographical sketches, by Charles Dexter Cleveland. London: 1868.

Hymns Ancient and Modern. With annotations, originals, references, authors' and translators' names, &c. Re-edited by Rev. Louis Coutier Biggs, M.A. London: 1867.

Annotations of the Hymnal. Consisting of notes, biographical sketches of authors, originals, and references. By Rev. Charles L. Hutchins, M.A. Hartford, Conn.: 1872.

HYMNS AND POEMS, ORIGINAL AND TRANSLATED. By Edward Caswall. Second edition. London: 1873.

SPECIMENS OF THE RUSSIAN POETS, with introductory remarks. 2 vols. By John Bowring, F.R.S. London: 1823.

THE BOOK OF PRAISE. From the best English Hymn-Writers. Selected and arranged by Roundell Palmer. Cambridge: 1870.

THE SUNDAY BOOK OF POETRY. Selected and arranged by C. F. Alexander. Cambridge: 1865.

LYRA MYSTICA: Hymns and Verses on Sacred Subjects, Ancient and Modern. Edited by Rev. Orby Shipley. London: 1869.

HYMNS OF THE EASTERN CHURCH. Translated by Rev. J. M. Neale, D.D. London: 1862.

HYMNS AND POEMS FOR THE SICK AND SUFFERING. Edited by V. Fosbery. London: 1861.

THE HARP AND THE CROSS. Compiled by Stephen G. Bulfinch. Boston: 1857.

THE YEAR OF PRAISE. Edited by Henry Alford, D.D., Dean of Canterbury. London: 1867.

MEDIÆVAL HYMNS AND SEQUENCES. Translated by Rev. J. M. Neale, D.D. London: 1862.

LATIN HYMNS, with English Notes. By F. A. March, LL.D. New York: 1874.

SACRED LATIN POETRY. Edited, with notes, by Richard Chenevix Trench, D.D. London: 1864.

LYRA BRITANNICA: A collection of British Hymns. Edited by C. Rogers. London: 1868.

LYRA CATHOLICA. New York: 1851.

LYRA DOMESTICA. Translated from the Psaltery and Harp of C. J. P. Spitta, by Richard Massie. Boston: 1861.

LYRA ANGLICANA. Collected and arranged by Rev. Robert H. Baynes. Leipzig: 1868.

HYMNS AND MEDITATIONS. By A. L. W. London: 1870.

CHRIST IN SONG: Hymns of Immanuel. Selected from all ages, with notes. By Philip Schaff, D.D. New York: 1870.

THE HYMNAL NOTED. London.

THE PEOPLE'S HYMNAL. London: 1877.

HYMNS FROM THE GERMAN. Translated by Frances Elizabeth Cox. London: 1864.

SONGS OF THE SOUL: Gathered out of Many Lands and Ages. By Samuel Irenæus Prime. New York: 1874.

EASTER HYMNS. Compiled by J. E. C. Chapman. Boston: 1876.

NOW IS CHRIST RISEN: Poems for Easter-Tide. Compiled by S. L. N. Boston: 1876.

THE SPIRIT OF PRAISE. A Collection of Hymns Old and New. London.

LYRA ANGLICANA. Edited by Rev. George T. Rider. New York: 1865.

LYRA AMERICANA. Edited by Rev. George T. Rider. New York: 1865.

POETICAL WORKS of Giles Fletcher, Edmund Spenser, Richard Crashaw, George Sandys, George Wither, John Beaumont, Henry Vaughn, George Herbert, Robert Herrick, Christopher Harvey, William Lisle Bowles, James Montgomery, Henry Alford, Mrs. Hemans, William Cullen Bryant, Jean Ingelow, and Charles Kingsley; together with various hymn-books, &c.

www.ingramcontent.com/pod-product-compliance
Lightning Source LLC
Chambersburg PA
CBHW020305240426
43673CB00039B/710